ESTATE PLANNING FOR PET OWNERS

WHO WILL CARE WHEN YOU'RE NOT THERE ?

D1445255

ROBERT E. KASS, JD, LLM
ELIZABETH A. CARRIE, JD, LLM

Illustrations by **Jill Flinn**

CAROB TREE PRESS, LLC
DETROIT, MICHIGAN

Copyright Notice

This book is available at special quantity discounts when purchased in bulk by educational institutions, corporations, organizations, or groups. For more information, please contact the publisher at the above address.

Cover design by SoroDesign, www.sorodesign.com

Illustrations by Jill Flinn, www.flinn-designs.com

Printed in the United States of America

ISBN 978-0-615-44340-9

WHAT PEOPLE ARE SAYING
ABOUT THIS BOOK

"This modest sized but beautifully illustrated book gives the pet owner an accessible discussion on how we all need to plan for the care of our pets if we should not be able to do so. The book is comprehensive, but structured in easily understood chapters that effortlessly set out the issues and the precise legal questions that everyone needs to answer. I have never seen as clear a road map to peace of mind for the future of our pets."

Professor David Favre, Michigan State University College of Law
Editor-in-Chief, Animal Legal & Historical Web Center, www.animallaw.info

"...An excellent, easy to use guide that will help you and your professional advisor develop a plan to care for your pet or service animal, such as a Leader Dog, if you are not able to care for them. Every day we witness how guide dogs enhance the lives of people who are blind and visually impaired. The beautiful illustrations are reminders of the love and companionship our animal friends bring to our lives."

Gregory Grabowski, President & CEO
Leader Dogs for the Blind, Rochester Hills, Michigan

"As a veterinarian, I see too many cases where a pet owner has died and the family is unable or unwilling to care for the pets. They want them euthanized or will just drop them off at an animal shelter. As a pet owner, is this really what you want for your pets? Take the time to read this guide to learn how you can easily prevent this tragic outcome."

Dr. Orit Rachel Szwarcman, DVM
Home-Vet, Huntington Woods, Michigan

WHAT PEOPLE ARE SAYING
ABOUT THIS BOOK

"We can never love our pets enough. Our hearts are intertwined with theirs. We have to give them the care they need to know that, although we may be absent, they are never abandoned. Those of us who heed the advice in WHO WILL CARE WHEN YOU'RE NOT THERE? will honor our pets in the present and the future."

Martin Scot Kosins, Author of MAYA'S FIRST ROSE, DIARY OF A VERY SPECIAL LOVE
A memoir of undying devotion for anyone who has ever loved and lost a pet

"We would all like to believe that we will outlive our loved ones, whether two- or four-legged. Unfortunately, that may not be the case. As an owner of dogs and horses, I believe it is absolutely critical that we make arrangements for the continued care of the precious animals with whom we have shared our lives. This book shows us why and how to do it, and is *must* reading for every pet owner."

Lynne Ellen
Novi, Michigan

"Bob Kass and Betty Carrie have succeeded in presenting a wealth of practical advice, in plain English, on all the issues every pet owner needs to know to plan for their pets' future.... something many people are concerned about, but don't do because they frankly don't know where to start... This book will also be an invaluable resource for lawyers interested in estate planning for pet owners."

Anna Marie Scott, Attorney
Chair, Animal Law Section, State Bar of Michigan

"Men have forgotten this truth," said the fox.
"But you must not forget it.
You become responsible, forever,
for what you have tamed...."

from The Little Prince
by Antoine de Saint-Exupéry

Disclaimer

This book is intended to provide general educational information regarding estate planning for pet owners. It is not intended as a substitute for legal, tax, accounting, financial, or other professional advice, and you must therefore not consider this book as your professional advisor in book form. While every effort has been made to provide accurate, current information on the subject matter, we cannot predict the ways in which the laws will change—and they will change—and court decisions, regulations, and administrative rulings may also be issued which may change the outcome in a particular case.

In addition, the facts of a particular situation are crucial to the outcome, and the conclusions described in this book might be different with even slight variations of the facts. Neither the authors, nor the law firm with which they are affiliated, nor the publisher shall have any liability or responsibility to any person or entity with respect to any loss or damage caused, or alleged to be caused, directly or indirectly by the information contained in this book. **If you do not wish to be bound by the above, you may return this book, in new condition, together with your original receipt, to the publisher for a full refund.**

About the Authors

ROBERT E. KASS is a tax attorney whose practice is heavily concentrated in the areas of estate planning and estate administration. An honors graduate of the University of Michigan Law School, he earned his Master's Degree in Taxation from New York University. A Fellow of the American College of Trust and Estate Counsel (ACTEC), Bob is a member of the Detroit law firm of Barris, Sott, Denn & Driker, PLLC, where he serves as Chairman of its Tax, Estate Planning & Probate Group. His practice is also heavily involved in charitable and planned giving techniques, and he is an active advisor and member of the Planned Giving Professional Advisory Committees of numerous local, national and international charitable organizations. Bob is also a Board Member and past Chair of the Speakers Bureau of LEAVE A LEGACY® Southeast Michigan.

A frequent and lively speaker on topics related to tax and estate planning, Bob has taught numerous courses for the Institute of Continuing Legal Education, which provides continuing education to attorneys in the State of Michigan. He has delivered many lectures to civic and professional groups, and has also appeared on the CNN and CNN/Financial Television networks and local cable television. Bob also has co-authored a highly acclaimed layman's guide to estate administration, WHAT DO WE DO NOW? A PRACTICAL GUIDE TO ESTATE ADMINISTRATION FOR WIDOWS, WIDOWERS AND HEIRS, which is used as course material in estate administration classes and has readers throughout the United States and as far away as Guam and the United Kingdom.

ELIZABETH A. CARRIE is a tax attorney whose practice spans taxation, corporate, partnership and limited liability company law, and estate planning and administration. Betty earned her Juris Doctor degree and her Master's Degree in Taxation from the University of Florida Frederic G. Levin College of Law. She is also a member of the Detroit law firm of Barris, Sott, Denn & Driker, PLLC, where she plays a key role in the firm's Tax, Estate Planning & Probate Group. Betty is also deeply involved in assisting start-up businesses through Detroit's Tech Town research and technology park, a business incubator.

A long-time pet owner, Betty's relationship with and dedication to her dog provided the impetus for this book, so that other pet owners could become aware of their responsibilities, understand the critical issues in planning for their pets' well being, and be prepared to implement practical solutions.

Both Bob and Betty are members of the Animal Law Section of the State Bar of Michigan. They take great pleasure in assisting their clients in developing customized plans for the care and welfare of their pets, including Pet Trusts, and also in helping them craft planned giving arrangements for the benefit of animal welfare and other charitable organizations. 🐾

About the Illustrator

JILL FLINN is a former art teacher, award winning professional artist, and animal rescuer. She and her husband live rurally and have taken in over 100 abandoned dogs and cats. They fund their own shelter through Jill's art work which is inspired by many of the animals they rescue. All are taken to vets to be neutered, spayed, and have their medical needs met. Several acres of their farm are dedicated to housing the ones who are not adopted. They have had as many as 42 dogs and more than 20 cats. Currently 23 dogs call their farm home.

These grateful creatures are the beginning of a circle of giving.
They need a home and care; the Flinns get them those.
The antics and stories of these wayward pets inspire Jill's mixed
media art, which is the sole source of funding for their shelter.
Just as a dog goes around in a circle before lying down
to get comfortable, her art work goes in a circle
to make abandoned animals comfortable.

2011 marks the 22nd year of Jill turning her art into kibble and vet bills.

Focusing on the lighter side of rescue, her pieces are meant to bring
a smile to the face of the viewer. The joy and appreciation shown
by the rescues radiate through the art work.

Flinn Designs
www.flinn-designs.com
Email: flinndesigns@gmail.com

Acknowledgment

We gratefully acknowledge the support of the various members of our
Tax, Estate Planning and Probate Team at Barris, Sott, Denn & Driker, PLLC,
who assisted in so many ways, including reviewing numerous drafts and
researching the finer points of tax law as it applies to Pet Trusts.
Special thanks to Hayley Rohn-Davé, Judy Meshefski and
Karen Merritt for their efforts, and to Sonja Kass for her keen eye as well.

We also wish to express our thanks to our fellow members at BSD&D,
for their continued support of our estate planning and administration practice
over the years. Their wisdom, creativity, and enthusiasm for the practice of law
have been contagious, and it is gratifying that they see the benefit in spreading
the word about the need for special estate planning for pet owners.

Thanks also go to those who encouraged the preparation of this work:
Dr. Paul Bloom, DVM, Pamela Brown, Lynne Ellen, Prof. David Favre,
Gregory Grabowski, Paul Kaye, Ph.D., Martin Scot Kosins, Anna Scott, Lewis Small,
and Dr. Orit Rachel Szwarcman, DVM. All of these people took the time to review the
draft and offer comments and encouragement, for which we are most appreciative.
The responsibility for any errors obviously remains with the authors.

We also wish to thank our illustrator, Jill Flinn, and our cover designer,
Cecilia Sorochin, for their talents and contributions, which we believe make this
book much more attractive than a typical legal guide. More than just lending their skills
to this project, they also related to the subject matter and put their hearts into it.

Finally, a word of thanks to the many clients who have entrusted their families'
estate planning and administration to our firm, who have permitted us to learn from
their experiences, and who have allowed us to share those lessons with the public at large.

Dedication

To Sonja, Adena, Elias, Jeremie and Sheri,
whose patience and support
of all of my projects is endless,
and to Corban Joseph:
"Welcome to the world, and may you
someday enjoy a four-legged furry pet! "

R.E.K.

To Lexy and her team of primary caregivers:
My parents, Bob and Anne, who watch her while I am away
(and sneak her treats);
her veterinarians, Dr. Paul Bloom, DVM, DACVD, DABVP,
and Dr. Aubrie A. King, DVM, and their wonderful staffs
who keep her relatively itch-free and in good health;
my sister, Lois, her personal chef, and my cousin, Kathleen,
who helps out at bath time. . . as they say,
"It takes a village."

E.C.

TABLE OF CONTENTS

Preface   i

Introduction   vii

1   Why Should You Plan for Your Pets?   2

2   Planning for Your Incapacity, Unexpected Absence or Emergencies   6

3   The Key Players in the Plan   14

4   What Level of Care Should Be Provided?   20

5   How Do You Pay for the Care?   24

6   The Legal Framework   34

7   Tax Considerations   42

8   Loss of a Pet Owner or a Pet: Grief Support   54

9   Memorialize Your Pet; Leave a Legacy   64

10   Closing Thoughts: How Do You Implement the Plan?   70

Appendices

A.   State Statutes on Pet Trusts   76

B.   Pet Card   86

C.   Sign for Residence of Pet Owner   88

D.   Pet Information Sheet   90

E.   Pet Trust Drafting Checklist   96

From the Will of Samuel Trevithuan, carpenter, of the Parish of Padstow, in Cornwall, England, dated November 26, 1729. The Will is now reportedly in the Registry of the Consistorial Court of the Bishop of Exeter: —

"Item. — I do give unto my dear wife or my daughter, or to whose hands soever he may come, one shilling and sixpence weekly, for the well-treating my old dog, that has been my companion through thick and thin almost these fifteen years. The first time that ever he was observed to bark was when that great eclipse was seen, April 22nd, 1715. I say, I do give one shilling and sixpence a week, during his life, for his well-meating, fire in the winter, and fresh barley-straw now and then, to be put in his old lodging, in the middle cage, in the old kitchen, to be paid out of my chattel estate, and forty shillings a year that I reserved to make me a freeman of the county; desiring and requiring all people and persons whomsoever, not to hurt or kill him that hath been so good a servant of a dog, for sense and tractableness to admiration."

From THE WORLD OF WONDERS: A RECORD OF THINGS WONDERFUL IN NATURE, SCIENCE AND ART (London, Paris & New York: Cassell, Petter, Galpin & Co, 1883), part I p. 39 , cited on The Pet Museum, http://thepetmuseum.blogspot.com/

Preface

LEXY'S STORY

I grew up in a family with pets of all kinds: a hamster ("PeeWee"), a turtle ("Touché"), a cat ("Boots"), and a mutt ("Mac"). With the exception of Mac who came to us from the Humane Society with a bad case of kennel cough and ultimately underwent two surgeries for torn tendons, pet ownership was relatively inexpensive and uneventful. I naively assumed that was how it always was. So when the opportunity arose to take in Lexy, a purebred German Shepherd, for free, I jumped at it. This is our story.

Lexy (a/k/a Lex) and I have been a pack of two for a little more than 10 years now. She is of "distinguished" lineage, her claim to fame being that she was bred by the same breeder who provides German Shepherds to the Osmond family. She quite possibly may also end up being one of the most expensive "free" dogs in history.

My brother and sister-in-law originally bought Lexy for protection. Lex is a beautifully marked, sable colored, smallish German Shepherd who is also quite shy and timid; not exactly qualities one seeks in a protection dog. She quickly became a family pet in a busy, and at times, chaotic household that included young children and an older dog, Kayla, a white Samoyed who I am convinced suffered from borderline personality disorder. (Lexy has one distinctly shorter ear after a losing encounter with Kayla.)

Lexy is a sensitive and loyal dog and was protective of my nephew, Mike, and later, my newborn niece, Hannah. At nap time, Lex would assume her post beside Hannah's crib, protecting her sleeping charge against all comers (including Hannah's Nana).

While she had a big heart, Lexy was not exactly what one would refer to as the sharpest knife in the drawer. To this day, she sometimes does not recognize my sister when she walks in the door. To even the most casual observer, it was clear that the limited training Lexy received had simply not sunk in. Couple that with the exuberance of youth and you have a recipe for disaster. In addition to regularly swiping unguarded food off the table, and running through (not out) the door, Lexy suffered from severe separation anxiety and was frequently destructive when left alone. As a result, she spent a considerable part of her early years locked in her cage (getting her into it was a two-person job).

The end of the line finally came when the family made a quick trip to the store and left the dogs home and Lex uncaged. They came home to find that she had destroyed the corner of the couch. She had to go. My sister-in-law lined up a friend with a house on a large lot who was willing to take Lexy in and let the kids come visit. I had just signed a new lease for my apartment and told them that I would take Lexy in a heartbeat if only I had a house. They waited me out and within a week of closing on my house, and with visions of Rin Tin Tin in my head, my cousin and I were on our way to Chicago to bring Lexy home.

The kids bid tearful goodbyes to Lex, my brother and sister-in-law loaded the cage into the back of the SUV, and handed me a book containing seemingly everything you could possibly want to know about the German Shepherd dog. Lexy jumped in, and we were off.

She was confused and, of course, anxious, although the Cheetos I tossed her way seemed to help. After four and a half hours on the road, we dropped my cousin off, and finally arrived home. I set up the cage in the living room, tossed in a treat, and a tee shirt my brother had worn so that she would have a familiar scent. Lex went in, took a quick sniff, grabbed the treat, and never went back. The cage came down and, in spite of my best efforts to keep her off it, she claimed the easy chair in my living room as her preferred sleeping spot (although initially, she was discrete enough to wait until I went to bed before ascending to her throne for the evening).

Within days of her arrival, we began training with "Uncle Dan," the dog whisperer of Livonia, Michigan. While she was never one of the class superstars, Lexy and I mastered the "heel" command —"stay" and "down" for anything more than 10 seconds were lost causes—and we were soon able to go on regular evening walks. She was now somewhat under control and well on her way to becoming a good canine citizen.

Lexy continued to be, and to this day remains, a very cautious dog. On more than one occasion while out walking, she would stop dead in her tracks at the appearance of an unexpected leaf in our path or cower behind me as a stranger approached. She also continued to have a distinct aversion to small white dogs. Nevertheless, we were a team. I was her person and she was my dog.

We settled into a routine. I would drop her at my parents on my way to work, she would hang out with my retired dad during the day, I would pick her up on my way home, and we would walk in the evening. Because of her separation issues, she rarely spent time alone. I had initially planned on having a pet door put into my house, but Lexy refused to go outside by herself. Except for evening thunderstorms and most of July (fireworks season) when she would take refuge under the coffee table (and I would sleep on the couch by her side), she calmed down and became a reasonably well-behaved dog. She was also my trusted pal. Lexy was relatively low maintenance in those days. All she needed was some company, her red rubber ball, and an occasional treat. That would soon change.

It started innocently enough, a series of repeated infections in her ears and other areas where one does not want to spread antibiotic ointment. Next, a minor emergency—after consuming a full bag of potato chips she had snatched off the counter while at my parents (some habits are hard to break), she developed a severe case of pancreatitis. After a brief stay at the vet for IV fluids and yet another course of antibiotics, things went back to normal. Little did I know that it was merely the calm before the storm.

Lexy began licking her feet and other "personal" areas with a vengence and developed a rather angry looking rash. She was successfully treated with steroids and antibiotics and the rash went away. It came back. We treated it again. It went away. . . and came back. Lexy's vet, Dr. King, suspected allergies and we pursued the low-cost version of allergy testing (blood work) which confirmed that she did have allergies. After yet another course of steroids (long-term use of which can lead to other problems), Dr. King suggested that Lexy be seen by a specialist, Dr. Bloom, for more comprehensive allergy testing and treatment.

Dr. Bloom started with a scratch test (complete with a shaved side and grid) and placed Lexy on a temporary diet of ostrich and sweet potato to determine whether she had a food allergy. My sister became Lexy's personal chef. I had ostrich shipped in (in case you are wondering, it's expensive) and bought sweet potatoes by the case. For at least a month, my sister cooked and packaged batch after batch of the ostrich and sweet potato mix as we slowly added Lexy's regular foods back into her diet. The smell that permeated the house (and one's nasal cavities) during meal preparation and packaging was nauseating.

The good news was that she didn't have any food allergies and could go back to her regular (and cheaper) diet of kibble. The bad news was that she was allergic to almost everything else—grass, trees, mold, and dust. We began weekly injections of a custom mixed allergy serum and Staph Lysate (to boost her immune system and desensitize her to staph infections), and continued to battle infections and allergy flare-ups with antibiotics, ointments, medicated shampoo and lotion.

It took a couple of years of regular visits, but we finally have the allergies under control. I still give her weekly allergy and Staph Lysate injections. Her occasional allergy flare ups are treatable topically. We have now settled into a new phase, complete with its own occasional medical crises and curiosities.

We'll never know for sure what happened (Lex isn't talking), but in early 2010 I think she semi-impaled herself on a protruding branch of arborvitae, opening up a wound on her side. Lex had not been herself for a couple of days and during a scheduled follow up visit with Dr. Bloom, I noticed part of what I thought might be a small skin lesion on her side and asked him what he thought it might be. He pulled out his electric clipper and began shaving away more and more of Lexy's coat to get a full view. The wound (about the size of a small egg) had scabbed over but looked awful. He told me that if we could keep her from licking the scab off, the wound might heal without need for surgery.

We left the office with medicated shampoo, ointment, latex gloves, and a protective plastic cone the size of a small satellite dish to keep her from getting at the scab. Never the most graceful of dogs, and now oblivious to her increased length and width, Lex became a four-legged battering ram — bumping into walls, tables, and people. She hated that cone, but stoically endured the indignity of wearing it when left alone as the wound healed. She bided her time and in an unwatched moment, managed to pull the scab off, leaving an open, ghastly wound. Fortunately, the wound had healed to the point where stitches were not needed. It ultimately took about a month for the wound to completely heal and Lexy has a noticeable scar on her side as a souvenir of her misadventure.

Next came another severe gastric episode—uncontrolled vomiting and diarrhea—that began on a Friday evening and continued throughout the weekend, requiring multiple visits to the emergency vet (in case you are wondering, the emergency vet is expensive and requires payment up front). Next, a yeast and bacterial infection on her feet that we treated with a long course of antibiotics and a series of 10 minute foot baths that required Lexy to stand in two baking dishes filled with a bleach/water mix (another two-person job). And most recently, what appears to be a staph infection that is resistant to her standard antibiotic.

At the age of 12 ½ , Lexy is now approaching the end of the 10 to 13-year average life expectancy for the German Shepherd dog. Her muzzle is peppered with grey, she is losing her hearing and has begun to develop fatty masses and other skin growths. There is a stiffness in her gait and she has slowed down, going from leaping into the back of my SUV, to walking up a ramp, to climbing in, with assistance, through the side door. Her regular vet has ruled out hip dysplasia (a common problem with Shepherds), but her hips are arthritic and she has lost muscle in her back legs. We have added daily doses of Rimadyl (an arthritis medication) to her allergy regimen and treat her with Tramadol (a pain reliever) on her bad days to keep her comfortable. Our long walks in the evening are now a thing of the past, although we can still take a short walk around the block on a good day.

Lexy now sleeps most of the day. At my parents' home she camps out by the door, continuing to protect them from the dreaded mail carrier (she has a perfect record—the carrier always retreats) or stays downstairs with them, reclining on her dog couch in their family room. When I arrive at my parents' home in the evening, I will usually find her in a deep sleep on her couch (occasionally, I will find all three of them asleep). If she is having a rough day with her hips, she will often choose to stay downstairs rather than climb the five stairs to come home with me. At our home, her preferred spot is next to the sliding glass door where she passes the day watching squirrels, rabbits, and birds on the deck, now content to chase them in her dreams.

All in all, it has been a good, albeit expensive, run. Over the course of our 10 years together, I have spent more than $30,000 on Lex's medical care. Has she been worth it? Without question, yes. In a quiet moment watching her sleep, I reflect on what we have been through and think about what's coming. The odds are good that I will survive her, but what if something happens to me? Who would take care of her? How would they pay for her care or know what to do?

I think of the words of the fox to the Little Prince, "You become responsible, forever, for what you have tamed. . . ." I don't think I ever tamed Lexy, but I am responsible for her care, forever. As her person, it's both my responsibility and privilege to ensure that she is provided for. That's what this book is about. ❧

Betty Carrie

Introduction
PETS AND PEOPLE

In the eyes of the law, they are simply property. But ask an owner about his or her pet and you are likely to hear a story about a faithful companion, trusted confidant, and source of unconditional love and acceptance. Animals enhance our lives.

The importance and contribution of animals, particularly companion animals such as dogs and cats, to our health and well-being are increasingly being recognized. Our pets accept us as we are. They provide us with a sense of connection, unwavering support, comfort, and solace during periods of extreme stress and transition, such as divorce or the death of a spouse. Pets alleviate loneliness, a growing problem as our population ages and we increasingly interact with others electronically rather than face to face.

Pets are particularly important to children who view them as friends and family members. A child faced with the serious illness or death of a parent will often confide in the family pet feelings they are afraid to share with others for fear of upsetting their ill or surviving parent. Interacting with and taking care of a pet can provide a child with love, structure, and purpose during a period when his or her life feels out of control.

Dogs are equally important to the physically challenged, whom they serve as leader dogs for the blind and assistance dogs for individuals with severely limiting disabilities. Through extensive training, dogs can be taught to pick up dropped objects, open doors, retrieve telephones in case of an emergency and other important tasks. In addition to helping their owners with the tasks of everyday life that most of us take for granted, these dogs provide companionship and help open up the world for their owners. By providing a focus for conversation, they facilitate conversation and connection with others.

Dogs (and sometimes cats) are used in health care facilities as therapy animals to lessen patients' fear, loneliness, and depression as they recover from illnesses and injury and go through rehabilitation. Unconditional acceptance from a visiting therapy dog provides a psychological benefit to a patient struggling with a physical or emotional infirmity about which he or she feels self-conscious. Stroking and petting a dog can lower a patient's blood pressure and encourage physical movement and interaction with others.

The variety of species being used as therapy animals in addition to dogs continues to grow (cats, rabbits, guinea pigs, llamas and chickens are also used), as do the purposes for which they are used. Therapy animals are being used in psychological counseling settings and in libraries with children needing a safe place to practice out-loud reading. Dogs' and cats' keen sense of smell are being used to help diagnose diseases such as cancer and to alert diabetic owners to a drop in blood sugar levels and epileptic owners to a pending seizure.

Pet Ownership in the United States

The American Pet Products Association (the "APPA") reports in its 2009-2010 National Pet Owners Survey that 62% (71.4 million) of all households in the United States own pets. Pet ownership in the United States (as well as the amount spent on pets) has steadily grown over the years:

Number of Pets Owned in the U.S. (millions)[1]

Year	Dogs	Cats	Birds	Horses
1991	52.5	57.0	11	4.9
1996	52.9	59.1	12.6	4.0
2006	72.1	81.7	11.2	7.3
2010	77.5	93.6	15.0	13.3

Statistics gathered by the APPA and reported on its website show the growth in the amount we spend on our pets from $17 billion in 1994 to an estimated $47 billion in 2010 broken down as follows:

Food	$17.56 billion
Supplies/OTC medicine	$11.01 billion
Veterinarian care	$12.04 billion
Live animal purchases	$2.21 billion
Pet services: grooming & boarding	$3.45 billion

Congress has even taken notice of the value of the human-animal connection. In 2009, Representative Thaddeus McCotter introduced a bill (HR 3501) providing a deduction of up to $3,500 per year for qualified pet care expenses. It isn't law yet, but at least Congress is considering it.

Providing for Our Pets

Who will take care of your pets if you can't? Who will care if you're not there? There are a number of common assumptions people tend to make about providing for their pets' care: (a) I will outlive my pet (check out the list of average life spans to see if that is realistic); (b) someone will step forward to take care of my pet; (c) money won't be a problem—either it won't cost that much, my pet's caregiver will pay, or someone will contribute.

Average Life Expectancy of Pet Animals

Animal	Life Span (Years)	Animal	Life Span (Years)
Amazon Parrot	50 to 80	Dogs	13 to 15
Boa Constrictor	23	Ferret	12
Box Turtle	123	Gerbil	5
Canary	20	Golden Hamster	4
Cats (indoor)	12 to 18	Horse	40
Cats (outdoor)	4 to 6	Macaw	70 to 80
Cockatiel	20 to 30	Painted Turtle	11
Dogs (large)	8.5 to 12	Rabbit	9

Our goal in this book is to help you identify options and address issues relating to the care of your pet when you are no longer able to do so.

The Humane Society of the United States reported in 2009 that an estimated 4-6 million dogs and cats are euthanized by animal shelters each year. That amounts to somewhere in the range of 11,000-16,000 animals per day. No doubt some of those are due to the death of the pet owner, or inability of the pet owner to continue to care for the pet for other reasons.

Does every pet owner need to plan for their pet? Yes, but not all to the same extent. Planning for a horse, parrot, an animal with special health issues, or a purebred will necessarily call for more detailed and formal planning than a plan for a gerbil.

This book will help you identify and think about the issues that should be addressed in providing for your pet's care. However, because state laws vary and every situation is different, we do not include sample documents in this book. In fact, for all but the simplest of cases, we recommend that you work with an experienced estate planning attorney with an interest in planning for pet owners and actively participate in the design of a customized plan that will address your pet's unique needs. Nobody knows your pet better than you.

If you've picked up this book, you are probably already a responsible pet owner and have likely thought about what would happen to your pet if something happened to you. In the chapters that follow, you will learn what needs to be done and how to do it. ☙

1/   Source for pet ownership data for the years 1991, 1996, and 2006 is U.S. Census Bureau, Statistical Abstract of the United States: 2011 (130th Edition) Washington, D.C., 2010. Data for 2010 is from ownership statistics gathered from the APPA's 2009/2010 National Pet Owners Survey.

"The greatness of a nation
and its moral progress
can be judged by the way
its animals are treated."

– *Mahatma Ghandi*

Chapter 1
WHY SHOULD YOU PLAN FOR YOUR PETS?

If you have pets and care about them, you should think about what would happen to your pets if something happened to you. Your unexpected absence could be caused by a not-so-unusual flight cancellation, delaying your return home for a day more, or a terrorist incident which shuts down the air transport system for several days.

You could go to the hospital for routine out-patient surgery, and encounter complications. An accident could put you in the hospital for days or weeks. Or you could become disabled or die. For whatever reason, your pets might find themselves without you—for a relatively short period of time, a longer period of time, or forever.

You may have a circle of close friends or family who are already prepared to take care of your pets if any of these events occur. They may know your pets, be familiar with their routine, food, and medication, and be sufficiently well funded to take on this responsibility. In that case, you may feel that you don't need to do anything to assure that your pets will be well taken care of should something happen to you.

However, after learning more, you may decide that your current arrangement is not sufficient to assure the proper level of care for your pets. The people you have chosen to receive your estate—your financial assets—may not be the best ones to take care of your pets. You may have never even discussed care of your pets with them, or perhaps you will decide that the care-giving responsibilities should be handled separately from the financial aspects of care-giving. You may have created an arrangement which is not legally enforceable, and your heirs may thus challenge what you have done.

Here are several red flags which might suggest it's time to give the matter some additional thought:

☐ You live alone with your pets. Regardless of any other considerations, you really should be thinking about who would come to their aid if something happened to you.

☐ You are no young pup yourself, or you have some serious health challenges facing you. Either way, if there's a good chance your pets will outlive you, it makes sense to think about providing for your pets' care.

☐ Your pets are young, or they have a long life expectancy based solely on the type of animal. The longer their life expectancy, the more likely they will outlive you and that some continued care arrangement will benefit them. Life expectancies of certain pet animals are provided in the Introduction, and in Chapter 5 (for various types of parrots). Also, the longer their life expectancy, the greater the likelihood they will have special medical needs.

☐ Your pets are already facing serious physical challenges. If special needs presently exist, then those needs should be clearly spelled out and, if necessary, financially provided for.

☐ You prefer to avoid disputes among your family as to who gets to care for your pets.

☐ You have an arrangement in your estate planning documents to provide for the care of your pets, but you haven't thought about the legal and tax aspects. Perhaps other issues should be addressed — but you aren't sure what those other issues might be. You want to make sure you get it right.

☐ You haven't done any planning with regard to your pets, and agree that it's best if your pets' care is not left to chance.

If any of these situations might apply in your case, and you care about your pets, you should definitely continue reading. ❦

"If all the beasts were gone, men would
die from great loneliness of spirit,
for whatever happens to the beast
also happens to man.
All things are connected.
Whatever befalls the Earth
befalls the sons of the Earth."

*— Chief Seattle of the Suquamish Tribe,
letter to President Franklin Pierce (1854)*

Chapter 2
PLANNING FOR YOUR INCAPACITY,
UNEXPECTED ABSENCE, OR EMERGENCIES

People often think of estate planning in terms of what will happen if they die. However, it is equally important to plan for what will happen in the event of your incapacity. As far as your pets are concerned, what will happen if you are unexpectedly absent should also be considered. You should also plan for emergencies such as natural disasters, which affect the entire household, including your pets.

Your unexpected absence, if relatively short, and emergencies, can be addressed by a series of practical steps. Your possible incapacity, on the other hand, will create a situation best dealt with by pre-planning with legal documents.

Planning for Your Unexpected Absence

What would happen to your pets if you didn't make it home from work today? Assume that you're alive but just delayed for an indeterminate period of time.

If you've created a network of family, friends, neighbors or co-workers, and if you're in a position to call them, that's probably what you would do. Here are some points to consider to make it easier for them to step in to care for your pets in your absence:

☐ Have you provided them access to your residence? Do they have a key or pass code to gain entry? If you prefer not to give a key, do they know who to contact for immediate access? If you have set a burglar alarm, do they know how to deactivate it?

☐ Does your caregiver know the pets and their specific routines, food and medicine requirements, physical accommodations, emotional needs and behavior issues? Consider leaving written instructions — much as you might for a babysitter — to make sure that everything is clearly spelled out and nothing is overlooked. (See Appendix "D," for a sample Pet Information Sheet.)

☐ If any equipment is involved, do they know where it is and how to operate it? Are written instructions available?

☐ If there are reserves of food or medicine, do they know where they are and how to access them?

☐ Make sure your pets have proper ID. A picture of your pet should be provided, and any distinctive traits should be identified. This will also help if a pet is lost.

☐ Leave copies of veterinarian records along with current veterinarian contact information.

☐ Do you have a Pet Card in your wallet so that someone knows that you have pets and who to call in the event of an emergency? (See Appendix "B" for a sample Pet Card.)

☐ Do you have a sign on your residence to indicate that there are pets in your apartment or house? (See Appendix "C" for a sample Sign for Residence of Pet Owner. A free Emergency Pet Alert sticker can also be requested through the ASPCA (American Society for the Prevention of Cruelty to Animals). Go to http://www.aspca.org/pet-care/disaster-preparedness/. They can also be purchased at your local pet supply store.

Planning for Emergencies

Emergencies can strike at any time, sometimes without warning: fire, tornado, hurricane and floods are common examples. You may be home or away from home. In either event, you should have an emergency plan in place, and here we'll address only those aspects of the plan that relate to your pets. In addition to those items covered above:

☐ Identify a shelter where your animals could be taken if necessary.

☐ Gather together necessary pet supplies so that they could be taken quickly in an emergency.

☐ Keep an extra set of your pet's veterinarian records—and make sure all vaccinations are always up to date.

☐ Determine which local hotels and motels allow pets and where pet boarding facilities are located. Research some outside your local area in case local facilities close. You should be aware that, except for service animals, pets are generally not allowed in emergency shelters out of concern for the health and safety of other occupants.

☐ Contact your local emergency management office, animal shelter, humane society, or animal control office for advice and information on preparing for an emergency affecting your pets. The American Veterinary Medical Association has prepared a comprehensive booklet on planning for animals in disasters, *Saving the Whole Family*, which may be downloaded from the AVMA website, at http://www.avma.org/disaster/default.asp#family.

Do You Have Large Animals?

If you have large animals, such as horses, sheep or goats, you have probably already thought about emergency planning. However, make sure you haven't overlooked any of the following:

☐ All animals should have some form of identification.

☐ In an emergency, you will probably want to evacuate the animals whenever possible. You should map out primary and secondary routes in advance.

☐ Arrange for vehicles and trailers needed for transporting and supporting each type of animal, as well as experienced handlers and drivers.

☐ Make sure that your destination can provide adequate shelter, food, water, veterinary care and handling equipment.

☐ If evacuation isn't feasible, you will have to decide whether to move your large animals to a shelter or turn them outside.

Planning for Your Incapacity:
Durable Power of Attorney for Pet Care

What would happen to your pets in the event of your incapacity? For these purposes, "incapacity" could have a very broad meaning. Certainly if a court declared you legally incompetent you would be incapacitated and at that point may want someone to take over the care of your pets. However, even if the situation doesn't call for court intervention, there could be circumstances where you are unable to care for your pets and would want to grant someone authority to take over for you.

For example, you might have some physical or mental illness which affects your ability to act rationally and prudently to handle your financial affairs, and which could also affect your ability to care for your pets. This could be something which progresses over time, or something which happens suddenly, such as a heart attack or stroke or an accident.

It may be a situation which occurs and then resolves itself. In other words, you could be unable to care for your pets for a while, then regain the ability to do so.

You may simply have disappeared or be unaccountably absent. When we draft Durable Powers of Attorney, we provide that these situations also trigger the authority of your Agent to act. Likewise, if you are incarcerated, or detained under duress and unable to effectively manage your property and financial affairs, you would probably want someone to be able to handle your affairs — including the care of your pets.

These situations are admittedly less common, but they do happen. Just look back through recent newspapers and you will find many examples. We have certainly seen them in our estate planning practice.

We would consider all of these situations to result in your disability for purposes of triggering authority of someone to handle your financial affairs. In these situations it is appropriate to have someone authorized to take care of your pets.

Your estate planning documents may have already given authority to someone to act on your behalf with regard to financial matters in the event of your incapacity. You might have done that in a Durable Power of Attorney or Revocable Living Trust. (If you only have a Will, that will be of absolutely no help in this situation, as a Will is only effective on your death.)

If you haven't authorized someone to act on your behalf, a family member or friend may have to file formal Court proceedings to have you officially declared incapacitated and have the Court appoint a "Conservator" for your property. Your pets would then be subject to the control of whoever takes control of your property.

If the Court has to appoint a Conservator, you may have little or no input into who takes care of your pets, the care provided and, perhaps most importantly, how much contact you and your pets would have with each other during the period of your incapacity.

Equally important, even if you have designated someone to handle your financial affairs in the event of your disability under a Durable Power of Attorney or Revocable Trust, is that the same person you would want to take care of your pets? (See the discussion on the differences between caregivers and financial responsibility in Chapter 3, "The Key Players in the Plan.")

Your general Durable Power of Attorney or Revocable Trust could be revised to specifically address care of your pets, and even appoint a different person as caregiver if that's your desire.

However, another document—a Durable Power of Attorney for Pet Care—can provide a more specific and extremely simple solution to this problem. In this document you would appoint the person you intend to serve as your pets' caregiver, with authority to do certain things related to the pets. This is nothing more than a very specific, and limited, form of Durable Power of Attorney, which should be prepared by your attorney after considering relevant issues, including the following:

☐ **Caregiver**: Who do you want to appoint as your "Agent" under this document? (See discussion of choice of caregiver in Chapter 3.) What if that person can't serve? Do you want to appoint a series of alternates?

☐ **Effective Date:** When do you want the authority to become effective? If it's effective when you sign the document—as opposed to making it effective only when you are incapacitated—that would allow the caregiver to step in immediately if you become disabled or are delayed. However, you will be giving current authority, and will have to trust your caregiver not to misuse that authority, for example, to withdraw funds from a specially designated bank account. (See discussion of finances in Chapter 5, "How Do You Pay for the Care?").

On the other hand, if you provide that the document only becomes effective upon your disability, then you will have to define how your disability will be determined. Sometimes that involves a process of obtaining one or more medical opinions, which would generally take time and might prevent the caregiver from acting as quickly as you might wish.

☐ **Scope of Authority:** How much authority do you want to give the caregiver? A broad grant of authority might state: "...to provide for the care of my pets, including food, shelter, health care, training and licensing."

Several questions arise with regard to the scope of authority:

1. Should the caregiver be given authority and direction to have the pets euthanized in the event of a pet's terminal illness or a condition in which the pet's veterinarian recommends euthanasia?

2. Should the caregiver be given the authority to have the pets euthanized if the caregiver is unable to continue to care for the pets?

3. Should the caregiver be authorized, or perhaps directed, to find a substitute home for the pets?

4. Should the pets be placed with a pet shelter rather than euthanized, or should placement with a shelter be prohibited?

5. Should the caregiver be given the authority to dispose of the pet's remains upon its death, or do you prefer to give specific instructions?

These issues are addressed in further detail in the Pet Trust Drafting Checklist (Appendix "E"). Many of the same issues arise, whether you are granting authority under a Durable Power of Attorney for Pet Care or a Pet Trust.

There is no "right" answer to these questions, and in our experience different clients have answered them differently, depending on their own personal feelings and experiences.

However, making sure that your pets are cared for in the event of your disability or unexpected absence is just as important as providing for them after you are gone. Addressing this situation will require thinking about who will care for the pets, the extent of the care, and who will take care of the financial side. It is all necessary to assure that you have fulfilled your responsibility as a caring pet owner. ❧

"All of the animals
except for man know that
the principal business of life
is to enjoy it."

— *Samuel Butler*

Chapter 3
THE KEY PLAYERS IN THE PLAN

In the human world, when an individual becomes unable to make decisions regarding his or her care or effectively manage his or her finances, a court will sometimes be called upon to appoint a *guardian* to provide for the person's day-to-day physical care, and a *conservator* to manage the person's finances. Both the guardian and the conservator will be required to regularly report back to and be accountable to the court for services provided to or for the benefit of the incapacitated person. In planning for your pet, you will need to fill those same three roles by providing for a *caregiver* (your pet's guardian), a *money person* (your pet's conservator), and a *watchdog* (the equivalent of the court).

The players you will need to involve in your plan will vary depending upon the number and types of pets you have, the needs of those pets, and the amount you plan on setting aside for their care. At a minimum, every plan should have at least one named caregiver and at least one, and preferably two, alternate caregivers who will step in to serve in the event your first choice is or becomes unable to serve for the duration of your pet's life. In a simple situation not involving a significant amount of money, the roles of caregiver and money person may be filled by the same person, with the watchdog role being filled by another family member or your pet's veterinarian. However, if you are planning on setting aside a sizable sum of money for your pet's care, we recommend that you put a more formal check and balance system into place by naming a person or institution other than the caregiver to handle the finances.

While the focus of this chapter is on selecting permanent caregivers, as you learned in the last chapter it is also important to have temporary or emergency care arrangements in place for your pet. The temporary caregiver may be a family member, friend, or even a neighbor who would be willing to take care of your pet during your absence or until a permanent caregiver is appointed. The same considerations discussed below that apply in selecting a permanent caregiver should be applied to selection of a temporary caregiver.

The Caregiver

The most important and difficult decision you will need to make in providing for your pet is selecting its caregivers. Your pet's caregiver will be making all decisions regarding your pet's care, including your pet's veterinary care and euthanasia. It is essential that you clearly discuss with the potential caregiver your expectations regarding your pet's care. Depending upon the life expectancy of your pet and the age of the caregiver, assuming the role of caregiver could end up being a lifetime commitment. Before naming any person to fill this role, you need to feel comfortable that person understands the responsibilities he or she will be taking on. You will also want to make sure that your pet and the potential caregiver spend some time together to ensure that they are compatible and that if the caregiver is also a pet owner, all of the animals get along.

The following situations raise additional concerns that need to be addressed:

1. Do you have several pets? If so, you need to determine whether your pets should stay together or whether different pets should go to different people. For the emotional well-being of your pets, it would be beneficial to keep pets together that have bonded; however, that may simply not be feasible. While someone, particularly if he or she is already a pet owner, may be willing to assume the responsibility of another animal, taking on more than one pet may be too much to handle.

2. Do you own an exotic pet or other animal requiring an owner with specialized skill and knowledge, e.g., a horse? If so, it is especially important that you name an individual with knowledge about the species and experience in caring for that type of animal.

3. Does your pet have any medical conditions, e.g., epilepsy, allergies, or arthritis, requiring special medical care? If so, you will want to be sure that your caregiver is capable of addressing your pet's medical issues and is fully briefed on your pet's challenges and the likely progression of these conditions as it ages.

4. Do you own a purebred animal that you breed? If so, you will need to clearly express your expectations regarding the breeding of your animal. Should you desire to continue to allow your pet to be bred, you want to be sure your caregiver understands and has experience breeding animals and, for your pet's health and the preservation of your pet's bloodline, will breed your pet responsibly.

5.   Does your pet have a long average life expectancy, e.g., a macaw (life expectancy 70 to 80 years)? If so, the appointment of alternate caregivers becomes even more important. You should also plan for the possibility of your pet surviving all of your named caregivers.

What if you can't identify anyone to serve as your pet's caregiver or your pet outlives all of your named caregivers? You may have to consider placing your pet with an animal sanctuary specializing in the long-term care of aged, abused, or displaced animals, or an organization specializing in the placement and adoption of pets. (See discussion of prepaying for your pet's care in Chapter 5, "How Do You Pay for the Care?")

It is important to visit the facility you are considering before the need arises in order to see what your pet's living arrangement would be, how it would be cared for, the level of socialization and exercise your pet would receive, as well as the organization's operating policies and procedures. Your pet's veterinarian can be a valuable source of information in this situation. You may also want to authorize the Trustee of your Revocable Trust or the Pet Trust to place your pet with a suitable caregiver. However, if substantial sums of money are involved, you will not want to give the Trustee the authority to appoint himself or herself as caregiver unless he or she steps down from the role as Trustee. If you don't want to leave the decision to the Trustee, you could establish a panel made up of friends, family members, and a veterinarian for that purpose.

The Money Person

As we have seen, it is important that you select someone who is qualified and who you trust implicitly to serve as your pet's caregiver. It is equally important that you make sure that sufficient financial resources are available to that person to provide for your pet's care and that those financial resources are effectively managed. (See Chapter 5 for a discussion of how much is enough.)

It goes without saying that the person you appoint to manage the finances should be experienced in handling money and be trustworthy. A family member or friend with financial acumen can be a good choice. As you will do in naming a caregiver, you should also appoint one or more Successor Trustees to step in as Trustee in the event your first choice predeceases your pet or chooses to step down.   If you are setting aside a significant sum of money for your pet's care, you may wish to name a bank or financial institution as Trustee and provide a trusted family member or friend the authority to replace the institutional Trustee with another financial institution or other independent Trustee.

The Watchdog

While you will do your best to pick trustworthy, responsible persons to serve as caregivers for your pets, you should also consider requiring the Trustee to serve as a watchdog to make sure your caregiver is performing his or her duties. You could also name another independent person, or an animal care panel made up of trusted friends, family members and one or more veterinarians, to serve this function. Within the actual Pet Trust you can also formalize this watchdog position (and expand it to allow for oversight of the Trustee) by providing for a Trust Protector. It would be this person's job to make sure that your intentions in creating the trust for your pet are being carried out.

At a minimum, your caregiver should be required to have your pet examined by a veterinarian (preferably, your pet's regular veterinarian) at least annually to monitor its health. You should also require your watchdog to make regular inspections of your pet, at random times, to assess its living conditions and its physical and psychological health. If the care of your animal will require boarding or the involvement of third parties in addition to your caregiver, such as in the case of a horse, you should give serious thought to establishing an animal care panel and having them provide for periodic, unannounced visits to the facility at which your animal is being boarded to ensure it is receiving proper care.

You also need to be sure that your plan gives your Trustee or animal care panel the authority to immediately remove your pet from any facility or the possession of any caregiver if, in their sole discretion, they feel your pet is in danger or not being properly cared for, and to deliver your pet to an alternate caregiver. Finally, in situations requiring the management of large sums of money, the Trustee or other money person should be required to provide annual accountings to the animal care panel, Trust Protector, or some other independent person.

Compensation

In all but the simplest of cases, your pet's caregiver should be reimbursed for expenses incurred in caring for your pet. You may want to do this by way of direct reimbursement by the Trustee upon presentation of receipts for expenditures. However, this could prove to be cumbersome and the caregiver might not want to front pet care expenses. Alternatively, you could provide for a budget, which should be subject to adjustment for inflation, or by the Trustee or animal care panel after consultation with the caregiver. The caregiver would then be paid a fixed amount on a monthly or quarterly basis, with additional distributions for extraordinary expenses in excess of budgeted amounts. You might also consider giving the caregiver a debit card to use to make purchases for the pet's care.

In addition to reimbursing expenses, you should also consider compensating your pet's caregiver, for taking on the responsibility of caring for your pet and to encourage your caregiver to continue in that role. A caregiver's right to compensation (as well as the right to receive budgeted care allowances) should be contingent upon providing proper care for your pet. In addition, care should be taken to ensure that the compensation paid is reasonable in order to avoid creating an incentive for the caregiver to needlessly prolong the life and suffering of your pet should it become terminally ill (or possibly obtain an identical replacement for your pet should it die or be lost). While it might seem logical in some cases to provide that any money remaining in the Pet Trust at the time of its death be distributed to the caregiver, consider if this might create an incentive for the caregiver to accelerate your pet's death in order to receive the balance of the trust. Leaving the balance to a charity, perhaps an animal welfare organization, would eliminate that incentive.

Your Trustee or other money person should also receive a stipend for his or her services commensurate with the level of responsibility assumed and the services provided. A bank or financial institution serving as Trustee may well charge a fee based upon the amount of assets under management. Your watchdogs should also be reimbursed for expenses they incur in monitoring your pet's care and, if appropriate, might also receive a small stipend for their services, or possibly no stipend at all if they are merely providing occasional oversight. Finally, if you are enlisting the services of your pet's veterinarian to serve on an animal care panel or otherwise serve as a watchdog, he or she should be compensated at his regular professional rates. 🐾

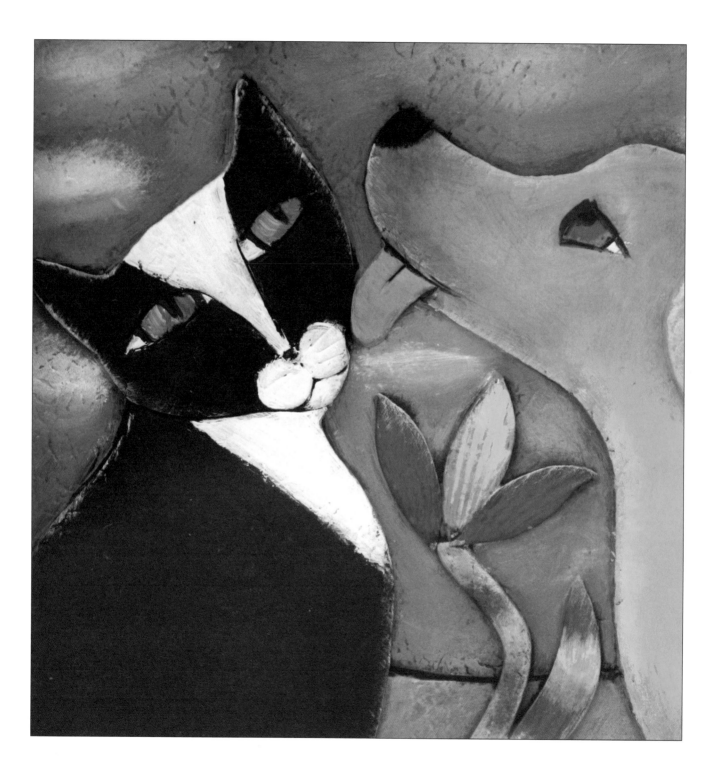

Chapter 4

WHAT LEVEL OF CARE SHOULD BE PROVIDED?

It is vitally important that emergency personnel and your pet's designated caregivers have immediate access to information about your pet. Otherwise, your pet could get lost in the shuffle in the period immediately following the time you die or become unable to care for your pet, particularly if the event giving rise to your incapacity or death is unexpected.

Pet owners should carry an animal notification card in their wallets providing the following information for each pet: (a) the pet's name, (b) the type of animal it is, (c) the pet's location, and (d) the names and contact information of the pet's emergency caregiver and veterinarian. (See Appendix "B" for a sample Pet Card.) You should also make sure that the people you are listing are aware of or know where to find any information regarding special care or medication your pet requires. Not to be overly dramatic, but assuring this information gets into the hands of the right people in a timely manner can literally mean the difference between life and death for your pet.

The Caregiver's Guide

After the immediate crisis has passed and the care of your pet is ready to be taken over by its permanent caregiver, you will want to be sure that person has the information he or she will need to make your pet's transition to its new home go smoothly. Remember, nobody knows your pet as well as you do. So even if you have chosen someone who already knows your pet to serve as its caregiver and have previously discussed your expectations regarding your pet's care with that person, you will want to create a "guidebook" for your caregiver to follow in which you lay out, in detail, information regarding your pet's health history and care including the following:

☐ Your pet's medications (including the required dosages and directions for their administration).

☐ Any special dietary concerns, the brand of and type of food (and treats) it likes and its feeding schedule.

☐ Your pet's physical and emotional needs. For example, how much exercise does your pet need? What is your pet's general activity level and does it have any special physical challenges? Is your pet outgoing or timid? Does it have favorite toys?

☐ Behavioral and temperament issues. For example, does your pet get along with other animals and children? Does your pet suffer from separation anxiety? Is it afraid of thunderstorms? Has it ever had problems with aggression or attacked a person or other animal? (The Trustee of your Pet Trust should be permitted to use trust money to purchase liability coverage to protect the caregiver and the Trustee from any damage your pet may cause to property or other persons).

☐ Contact information for your pet's regular care providers, e.g., veterinarian (regular, and if applicable, veterinary specialists with whom it is treating), groomer, dog walker, trainer, and, if applicable, where you board your pet while on vacation.

In short, this document should include everything you would want to know if you were in the position of having to take over your pet's care. See the Pet Information Sheet in Appendix "D" as an example. If your pet requires specialized care or has other special needs, you should also consider preparing a "day in the life" video that your pet's caregiver can refer to in carrying out your instructions.

Thinking About the Unthinkable

As pet owners, none of us like to think about the possibility of having to put our pet down. However, this is one issue you need to tackle head on in connection with a Pet Trust, especially when your caregiver and others involved in caring for your pet have a financial interest either in keeping your pet alive (in order to continue to receive compensation) or in accelerating your pet's death (in order to receive the assets remaining in the trust).

As a general principle, your plan should direct your caregiver to obtain all reasonable veterinary care that your pet may need to maintain and, if injured or ill, restore it to generally good health and to alleviate suffering, if possible. Your plan should directly address the possibility of your pet suffering from an injury or illness which is beyond the capabilities of reasonable veterinary medicine to cure. If your pet finds itself in a situation in which it is suffering from an incurable disease or an irreparable injury leaving it with a poor quality of life, what should be done? Your plan should include clear instructions regarding end-of-life issues and the prevention of needless prolonged suffering, including possible euthanasia, and require that decisions of this nature are made in consultation with your pet's regular veterinarian, by others you may indicate, or by your pet care panel, if you have provided for one.

Your plan should also provide instructions and funding for the final disposition of your pet's remains after it dies. This can be as simple as allowing your pet's veterinarian to provide for the cremation and disposal of your pet's ashes. Other options include having your pet cremated and placing its ashes in an urn or scattering them, or providing for the burial of your pet in a pet cemetery. (For more on memorializing your pet, see Chapter 9.) ❦

Chapter 5

How Do You Pay for the Care?

After you have decided that you need to provide for your pet's care and have figured out who will be the caregiver, you should determine how much you should set aside, and how and when you will do it. This is called "funding." Funding means transferring money or other property into your trust so that money is available to take care of your pet. Without adequate funding, the Trustee will not be able to take care of your pet after you die, unless the Trustee takes funds from his or her own pocket, which we assume is not your intent.

How Much Is Enough?

How much to provide will depend greatly on the type of animal and life expectancy of your pet, and what you think is reasonable (the standard of living you want to maintain for your pet), probably based in large part on what you have spent in the past. You should also consider whether you wish to pay a fee to your caregiver for his or her services, and/or to the Trustee if your plan includes a Trustee. Caregivers and Trustees are not always compensated, but sometimes they are.

For example, here's an estimate of what would be necessary to care for a pet parrot on an annual basis:

Food	$400
Toys and other supplies	$500
Pet-sitting during vacation	$300
Veterinary checkups	$300
Total per year	$1500
Plus cages (every five years)	$500

Taking the parrot as an example, the above figures should be multiplied by the pet's longevity:

English Budgie:	7 years
America Budgie:	14 years
Cockatiel:	20-30 years
Parrotlet:	20-25 years
Lorikeet:	20-30 years
Quaker Parakeet	30 years
Conure:	30 years
African Grey Parrot:	50 years
Amazon:	50-80 years
Blue & Gold Macaw:	70 years
Other Large Macaws and Cockatoos:	80 years

You may also want to add a factor for potentially expensive medical treatment.

Every pet and every situation will be different. You should carefully consider costs which could occur in your case, which might include some or all of the following:

☐ Extraordinary medical treatment.

☐ Pet health insurance.

☐ Grooming.

☐ A pet-sitter or professional boarding when your caregiver might go on vacation, travel out of town on business, be hospitalized, or may be temporarily unavailable to care for your pet personally.

☐ Expenses for travel if your pet is to accompany the caregiver on vacations.

☐ Extra expenses to take care of your pet's end of life situation, including costs which may be involved if your pet has to be put to sleep, costs of any burial or cremation, and memorials.

☐ Fees for your pet's caregiver and/or Trustee.

If you have the funds (or will have sufficient assets at the time of funding), it may be better to overestimate rather than underestimate, and particularly if whatever is left will be going to your favorite animal charity. (See Chapter 9, "Memorialize Your Pet; Leave a Legacy.")

Sometimes pet owners with large estates will set aside a very large amount, with the intent to use only the income to pay the expenses, and principal to be used only for exceptional expenses. If your estate is relatively small, then perhaps transfer of a lesser amount will be appropriate, with the notion that the funds will be used regardless of whether they are income or principal.

Whatever your estimate, multiply the projected annual expenses by your pet's longevity, and add the one-time expenses, and this will give you some idea of how much you should provide to keep your pet in the style to which your pet is accustomed. This will not be a precise figure, because costs rise and life is unpredictable. If you have picked the right caregiver, he or she will be delighted to care for your pet, and the funding is just a target to avoid creating an undue burden.

Remember, also, that even if you anticipate outliving your pet, you may acquire another, and this type of planning should be done so it covers not only your present pet but also any pets which become part of your family in the future. That means that an estimate based on total life expectancy may be wiser than just planning for your present pet's remaining life expectancy.

Should You Just Fund A Very Large Amount to Avoid Under Funding?

Why bother with projections and estimates? Why not just leave your entire estate, or a very large amount, to fund your pet's care to make sure that funding will be sufficient?

In cases where other family members are already well provided for, a pet owner may certainly be tempted by this approach. However, it can be very risky. An extremely large gift, even if not the entire estate, is likely to encourage your heirs and possibly remainder beneficiaries—those who would receive your estate after the pet's death—to challenge your estate plan.

Courts have approached this differently around the country, but there is precedent for a court reducing the amount involved to an amount which the court deems sufficient to accomplish the pet owner's purpose.

Two "uniform laws" which have been adopted in various versions by various states specifically address this issue: The Uniform Probate Code, § 2-907(c)(6) (1993), authorizes the court to reduce the amount if it "substantially exceeds the amount required" to care for the animal. The Uniform Trust Code, § 408(c), provides that "[property] of a trust authorized by this section may be applied only to its intended use, except to the extent the court determines that the value of the trust property exceeds the amount required for the intended use." Summaries of state statutes on Pet Trusts which often contain the same provisions as these uniform laws are included in Appendix "A."

To see how this operates in practice, consider the following court cases:

In a 1974 case, *In re Lyon's Estate*, 67 Pa. D. & C.2d 474, 482-83 (C.P. Orphans' Ct. 1974), the court reduced the amount left for the care of animals to what the court considered reasonable. **Florence Lyon** had left a Will directing that principal or income from her estate should be used to take care of her six dogs and four horses. The residue of her estate was to be distributed to Princeton University.

When she died, it was estimated that the estate would generate in the range of $40,000-$50,000 per year. This appeared to be well beyond what would actually be necessary to take care of the animals. However, it also appeared that she did not know how large her estate was or what it would cost to care for her animals.

The court's approach to this situation is interesting: It determined that the life expectancy of the animals ranged from one to twenty years. The court estimated that it would take five acres of land, plus $22,000 for a shelter and $5,000 per year to take care of the animals. Based on those factors, the court concluded that the amount indicated by Mrs. Lyon for the animals was excessive, and it modified the Will provision to either establish a $150,000 reserve to be held for the care of the animals, or leave the entire residue to Princeton University with a proviso that it be responsible for the care of the animals.

In a more recent, well-publicized case, billionaire **Leona Helmsley**, who died in 2007, left most of her estate to a charitable trust. However, she also left $12 million to a Pet Trust for her Maltese poodle, Trouble. The Pet Trust was valid under New York law. However, this amount was subsequently reduced to $2 million by a Manhattan Surrogate Court judge, with the support of the New York Attorney General, with the $10 million going instead to her charitable trust.

Nine-year-old Trouble was sent to live in Florida with Carl Lekic, the general manager of the Helmsley Sandcastle Hotel, even though Mrs. Helmsley's brother, followed by a grandson, were designated under the Will to get the dog. Lekic, Trouble's caregiver, has stated that $2 million would pay for the dog's maintenance for more than 10 years, which is beyond Trouble's life expectancy. The annual costs to maintain Trouble include $100,000 for full-time security (several death threats have been received), $8,000 for grooming and $1,200 for food, plus a $60,000 guardian fee for Lekic. In addition to the $12 million Leona Helmsley left for Trouble, she left a Mission Statement with non-binding instructions that her charitable trust, which had been valued at $5-$8 billion, be used for the care and welfare of dogs, although the Trustees are not legally bound to follow those wishes.

If you are contemplating funding your Pet Trust with what anyone would consider an excessive amount, consult your attorney to see how best to support that amount. Otherwise, there is ample authority in the statutes and the case law for reducing it.

What If the Funding Is Insufficient?

If you don't fund with a sufficient amount, or if your projected investment returns are not realized, and the trust runs out of money before your pet dies, the Trustee will not have funds to pay for the pet's care. The Trustee will not be responsible to pay for your pet's care out of his or her own funds.

Depending on the relationship, and the caregiver's own circumstances, the caregiver may or may not want or be able to continue to pay for the pet's care from his or her own funds.

This is why proper funding of the Pet Trust is critical. Also, in the event the Pet Trust runs out of money, you should probably provide the name of the person or organization to whom your pet should be given. Otherwise, your pet could end up in a shelter and possibly euthanized.

What Are Typical Sources of Funding a Pet Trust?

Your Pet Trust can be funded from various sources. The possible sources and timing of the funding will depend to a great extent on the legal framework you choose for your Pet Trust. If you decide to create the arrangement during your lifetime, it could be funded during your lifetime or after your death. However, if you decide that the arrangement should only go into effect after your death, then the funding would not generally occur until after your death, though you could set up a joint account, for example, during your life which will only pass to the intended person after your death. (See below for risks of joint accounts.)

Partial funding to be supplemented by additional funding later is also possible. For example, if you have a lifetime Pet Trust, you might set up a bank account with a relatively small amount to cover the costs of your pet's care for a relatively short period of time. This would avoid the initial delay in making the arrangement operational.

Additional funding could come into the trust after your death. For example, it could come from a nonprobate asset, such as a special bank account naming the Trustee of the Pet Trust, as "pay on death" (POD) or "transfer on death" (TOD) payee. This is safer than a simple joint account, where the person would actually be able to withdraw the money for some other purpose, even during your lifetime. The joint account could also be the target of creditors of the joint owner in the event of a lawsuit totally unrelated to you or to your pet's care.

You may also consider naming the Trustee of the Pet Trust as the beneficiary of life insurance on your life, or as beneficiary of a percentage of the death benefits if the total death benefits under a given policy would exceed your desired funding amount for the Pet Trust. If you do that, however, make sure the beneficiary is properly named. The beneficiary should not be your pet! Your pet is not considered a person and cannot be the direct beneficiary of life insurance proceeds. Ask your attorney for the proper way to name your Trustee as the beneficiary. One typical method would read as follows: "John Jones, as Trustee of the Cindy Smith Pet Trust under Trust Agreement dated [the date of the trust], and his Successor Trustees."

In general, however, you would not want to name the Trustee of the Pet Trust as the beneficiary of IRA or retirement plan benefits. This is because those benefits will be subject to income taxation as withdrawn, which will affect the amount available for your pet's care. Further, if the trust is the beneficiary, the benefits may have to be withdrawn faster (possibly within five years after your death), than if another beneficiary (a person) was the beneficiary, where the benefits may qualify for withdrawal over the beneficiary's life expectancy. One of the benefits of a tax-deferred retirement account, i.e., deferral of income taxes, may thus be lost. So if you have a choice between leaving IRA or retirement plan benefits to a Pet Trust or to an individual, talk to your attorney about which would be the best use of the funds in your particular case.

What if you don't have sufficient liquidity, i.e., cash or marketable securities, to fund your Pet Trust during your lifetime, or to segregate in a separate account for distribution after your death? You can simply wait until your estate is settled, and assets are sold, and the specified dollar amount can be transferred to your Pet Trust at that time. This may not be the best solution, because there could be delays in selling assets, but you may not have a choice.

What About Prepaying For Your Pet's Care?

If you do not have someone who can be your animal's caregiver and/or Trustee of your Pet Trust, then it may be possible to find a long-term care facility which will provide your pet care for life. Note, however, that you are embarking on a difficult journey. Most humane societies do not have space or funds to care for your pet for the rest of its life. Further, they cannot guarantee that your animal will be adopted. Some will be able to care for your pet on a temporary basis until the animal is transferred to your designated caregiver, but that is a totally different arrangement than long-term care. There are, however, organizations which provide long-term care for pets whose owners who have passed away. These are sometimes referred to as "pet retirement homes" or "sanctuaries."

Ask your veterinarian or local humane society for recommendations of pet sanctuaries or retirement homes. You can also do a Google search using the following words: animal retirement home, or search for lists of these organizations by using the following search: list pet sanctuaries. Also consider breed rescue groups, which generally deal with purebred dogs and cats, but sometimes also take mixed breeds. Some of those will care for the pet and try to find it a good home. Your humane society may be able to help you find such a group. The Michigan Humane Society, for example, has an online search engine to help you find a rescue group by breed, and some of those have members and affiliates nationally. See http://www.michiganhumane.org/ and look under Pet Resources / Surrendering An Animal, for the link to the Breed Rescue Group search engine. Read about the organization on its web site to understand its mission and how it operates.

Some may agree to find your pet a new home, and some will even commit to care for your pet for the rest of its life.

If you are considering this type of alternative, and particularly one where care and not adoption is the goal, you should carefully evaluate numerous issues:

☐   Most pets are companion animals which need a significant amount of personal care and attention, not just room and board. Will your pet thrive in this type of situation on a long-term basis? Will your pet receive the desired level of human interaction and level of care?

☐   Will the organization actually care for your pet? Is it possible that they will just find a foster home for your pet and is this acceptable to you? In that event, would the fee or contribution you pay be based on long-term care or a short-term stay prior to adoption?

☐   What are their policies regarding placement with a new family?

☐   What will actually happen if the organization runs into financial difficulties? How long have they been in existence, and what is their track record? Are any references available, such as from animal organizations, which can give you the required level of comfort? Is there any way to check for possible complaints against the organization? If the organization is a non-profit, see if they are listed in GuideStar, a watchdog organization. http://www2.guidestar.org/

We highly recommend that you contact several organizations that you are considering, gather information about their programs, and visit their facilities. You need to see, first hand, how they are caring for the animals entrusted to their care. See how they are confined, who is looking after them, and the degree to which they have human interaction and are exercised. You might also check with the Better Business Bureau to see if there are any complaints.

Make sure to have your attorney review any contracts that are presented, as well as the financing options. Financing alternatives can vary, and may include:

☐ A one-time lump sum payment to cover all future care of the pet during its lifetime.

☐ Designation of life insurance proceeds to cover the care.

☐ Setting up a charitable remainder trust to make the annual payments.

☐ Leaving a bequest in your Will or Revocable Trust to cover the costs.

If you decide to use one of these organizations, share that information with your friends, relatives and neighbors. Otherwise it is possible that a well-meaning friend or relative will take possession of the animal without even being aware of what you have provided in your estate planning documents or by contract. This could cause much confusion and disappointment, and might even result in your beloved pet ending up in the middle of a dispute, and subjected to unnecessary anxiety and suffering.

Most pet owners will probably not like the idea of their pet living in a clinic or shelter setting. But some people will find that the right organization provides the best, and perhaps, the only alternative in their situation. 🐾

Chapter 6

THE LEGAL FRAMEWORK

If you have ultimately determined that you wish to appoint a caregiver for your pet, and if you're not sure if you want to simply rely on an informal arrangement, then you need to understand how to make a formal arrangement. The good news is that you have several options, and you should understand the implications of each of them before making a decision.

Care While You Are Living

The Durable Power of Attorney for Pet Care (discussed in Chapter 2) is intended to take care of situations where you are alive but for some reason cannot take care of your pet yourself. When we say that a Power of Attorney is "durable," that means it continues in effect during a period of your disability. However, the power that you give under that document will terminate upon your death. So while it may be useful to have that document in place, it will only take you so far.

We believe that the Durable Power of Attorney for Pet Care offers significant advantages over informal arrangements. For example, you may talk to a neighbor, friend or family member, and have some sort of unwritten understanding that this person will take care of your pet if something happens to you. This agreement may not be legally binding, and most likely you would not be leaving any money for the person who is supposed to take this responsibility, or if so it may be intended to cover a very short term situation, which could turn out to be longer. If it is not legally binding, others in the family may interfere, thwarting your intentions as pet owner.

Informal arrangements may be very loose, and may not include specific instructions as to the care to be provided, and what will happen if the caregiver can no longer care for the animal. While informal arrangements are probably very common, if you are taking the trouble to plan for your pet's care after your death, with some level of formality, we strongly suggest that you do the same to cover the situation where you are alive but for some reason cannot take care of your pet yourself.

The most effective method of handling care during your lifetime and after your death is probably a combination of the Durable Power of Attorney for Pet Care and a lifetime Pet Trust, discussed below. These could provide a seamless transition of care for your pet.

Care After You Are Gone

The informal arrangement has the same disadvantages in terms of providing care after your death as it does during your disability or absence. However, the situation will likely be aggravated because the period of time for providing care will presumably be longer post-death than during a period of your disability. The impact of a possible lack of specific instructions, successor caregivers, and funding, all make the informal arrangement the least desirable way to provide for your pet's care after your death.

As you consider the options, you should realize that the legal system does not see pets in the same way you do. Under the law, pets are generally classified as personal property, and if you don't deal with them specifically in your estate plan they may be handled in the same way as a sofa or a TV. Further, the courts in most cases will have the ability to reduce whatever dollar amount you may leave for your pet's care if the judge considers it excessive. Check your particular state statute to see how it addresses this situation, and keep it in mind as you design your arrangement for your pet's care. (See Appendix "A," State Statutes on Pet Trusts.) Here are what we consider the principal options:

1. **Outright Bequest.** You can simply leave your pet to someone who is willing and able to care for it after your death, in an outright bequest, possibly with a cash bequest to defray expenses.

2. **Testamentary Trust.** You could create a trust for your pet's care under your Will. These are called "Testamentary Trusts," and there are several types, which we will discuss below.

3. **Lifetime Arrangement.** You can create a lifetime arrangement, i.e., a Pet Trust which you create during your lifetime either as a free-standing document, or as part of a Revocable Trust, which you may already have in your estate planning.

Here are some of the differences between these approaches:

Outright Bequest of Pet and Cash

If you simply leave your pet and some cash to a person you have decided will care for your pet after you are gone, that may work, but it doesn't address what will happen if that person doesn't survive you. Also, what happens if your caregiver decides, for some reason, that he or she can no longer take care of the pet? This solution also does not address what will happen in the event of your disability, since a Will is effective only after your death. Also, if this will be contained in your Will, it will take some time to implement, as the Will has to be probated to be effective.

Leaving cash for your pet's care also raises an issue as to what you intend to be done with the money if it is not all used during the pet's lifetime. Do you intend that the caregiver should keep any balance? If not, then how will you assure that it passes to your intended beneficiary, perhaps an animal charity?

Is there any concern that the caregiver may simply keep the money and neglect the pet, give it away or abandon it? You may laugh about it, but people have been known to substitute another animal, a look-alike, for a particular pet after the pet's death, just so they could continue drawing compensation for the care of a pet. These days even cloning an animal is not impossible.

We are aware of a court case where a fellow was left $5,000 to take care of his uncle's pet cat, and after his uncle died he came to the Executor asking for the $5,000. When asked where the cat was, he said "I took care of it." The nephew had euthanized the cat! The court didn't agree with his interpretation of the Will and didn't order payment of the $5,000, but this points out the danger of outright bequests of cash—or even a bequest of cash conditional on accepting the pet—and the importance of selecting the right caregiver.

While selection of the appropriate caregiver is clearly essential, a trust can provide additional protection and could address all of above issues and appoint someone to supervise the trust and enforce its terms.

Trust Created Under Your Will (Testamentary Trust)

You can create a trust arrangement for pet care under your Will, a Testamentary Trust. However, as a general matter, Testamentary Trusts for pet care tend to provide short-hand solutions to problems which can be more fully addressed in a carefully considered lifetime Pet Trust.

Consider this language in a Will, which creates a Testamentary Pet Trust:

"I leave my dog, Fritz, to my niece, Betty Smith, along with the sum of $5,000 which I intend but do not require that Betty use to take care of Fritz for his lifetime."

Would this create a trust for the care of Fritz? Yes. Would Betty be required to use the money to take care of Fritz? No, because the language merely expresses an intent, which is specifically non-binding, probably so it would not be taxable compensation to Betty. Would it be the best solution? Consider these implications:

☐ A Testamentary Trust will only be effective after your death, as compared with a Revocable Trust which is effective when you sign it. Since the Testamentary Trust would only be funded after the Will is probated, funds might not be available for your pet's care during the delay period. Even if the probate process goes smoothly, it could still take some time. Also, your caregiver would not receive formal authority to take care of your pet immediately upon your death. This could lead to a delay in putting the arrangement into effect. In many cases, the Will is not even located or read until some time after the burial.

The delay may be short (several days), or it could be very long (several weeks or months), depending on state practice and whether the Will is contested. A Will contest, which could involve the provisions for the pet or other totally unrelated issues, could drag out administration of your estate for a considerable period of time.

☐ Depending on applicable state law, it may be easier for someone to challenge a Will and thus challenge a Testamentary Trust, than it is to challenge a Revocable Trust.

☐   A Testamentary Trust would not be effective on your disability, since a Will is effective only on death. A Pet Trust within a Revocable Trust, or created as a freestanding arrangement, would be effective on your disability.

☐   In a state without a specific statute making a trust for an animal enforceable, the Pet Trust created under a Will is an "Honorary Trust," which merely *authorizes* someone to take care of your pets, and leaves them some money to do that. The person is not *required* to provide the care (even if the language doesn't express non-binding intent but simply says "to take care of Fritz..."). The Trustee could transfer the funds back to the Executor or Personal Representative of your estate, who in turn would distribute the funds back to those people who receive your personal property.

☐   You may be able to create a so-called "Statutory Pet Trust."   This is allowed under the laws of certain states. In those states the trust would be legally enforceable by allowing the caregiver designated by the terms of the trust to force the Trustee to use trust funds solely for the benefit of the pet and payment of fees.

☐   Detailed care instructions are generally not included in a Will. The Testamentary Pet Trust generally does not provide for the types of contingencies that a fully considered Pet Trust would provide.

☐   Typically the person who is named in a Will to provide care to a pet would not be signing anything to accept those future responsibilities.

Thus, while your intent may be to provide for your pet, the opposite may result: Your beloved pet may end up without the care you expected would be provided.

It is certainly possible that an informal arrangement could be put into place while the Will is being probated, assuming everyone cooperates and if the caregiver is willing to advance funds and claim reimbursement from the trust when the trust is funded. However, an arrangement which has no inherent delays in granting authority or in funding can provide greater peace of mind for the concerned pet owner than a Testamentary Pet Trust.

This is why we generally recommend a lifetime arrangement. If you are able to avoid the probate process entirely, that should result in faster implementation of your plan overall, including your Pet Trust, and lower costs of administration. You will also address a host of issues you would typically not include in a Will. You will have thought through all the issues, and given specific instructions.

Lifetime Trust

There are two basic approaches to creating a lifetime arrangement for the care of your pets after you are gone:

You can do it in a separate document, a free-standing Pet Trust, which deals only with care of your pets. It could be funded when you set it up, or partially funded at that time and provide for additional funding after your death. You would reserve the right to change it any way you wish, at any time. Since it is created in a free-standing document, the trust would actually come into existence when you sign the document. It would be a simple matter to fund it partially, with additional funding to come after your death.

Alternatively, if you have a Revocable Trust as part of your own estate plan, a Pet Trust could be incorporated into that trust. In that event the Pet Trust wouldn't actually come into existence until after your disability or death, and would not be funded at all until then. There could be some delays in funding, depending on how you plan to fund the trust.

Whether you use a free-standing Pet Trust or a Pet Trust incorporated into your Revocable Trust plan, the document would be operative without the necessity of Probate Court approval. This would thus avoid any delays which could occur if a trust is created under your Will.

Even though there are various state laws addressing pet trusts – the Honorary Pet Trust and the Statutory Pet Trust — and a few states do not have any laws on pet trusts at all, in every state a pet owner can create a Revocable Trust to care for a pet, i.e., a Traditional Pet Trust. ❦

"Dogs have given us their absolute all.
We are the center of their universe, we are
the focus of their love and faith and trust.
They serve us in return for scraps.
It is without doubt the
best deal man has ever made."

– Roger Caras

Chapter 7
Tax Considerations

No discussion of estate planning for pet owners would be complete without at least touching on the tax aspects of the types of planning which may be involved. For example, savvy pet owners will wonder whether and how they can take a tax deduction for the amount they will set aside for their pets on their death. Is it possible to create an estate tax charitable deduction?

If you create and fund a Pet Trust during your lifetime, are you making a taxable gift, perhaps to the person who is charged with your pet's care? Can you get an income tax deduction?

Will the trust itself end up paying income tax, or is there a way to make the pet taxable, as the "beneficiary" of the income? Or will the individual you put in charge of the money, for the pet's benefit, be considered the beneficiary and taxable on the income?

The answers to some of these questions depend on whether the Pet Trust is an Honorary Pet Trust, a Statutory Pet Trust, or a Traditional Pet Trust. The types of Pet Trusts available depend to some extent on state law. We've touched briefly on these different types of trusts in the previous chapter ("The Legal Framework"), but now we need to dig a little deeper so you get a better sense of the differences and, in particular, how they can affect taxation.

Honorary Trusts. In the past, many states permitted Pet Trusts but provided that they were not enforceable against the Trustee. Currently, Wisconsin is the only state that has a statute dealing with pet trusts but it is not enforceable. These are typically called "Honorary Trusts." This means that once a Trustee receives the funds for the care of your pet or other noncharitable purpose (e.g., care of a tomb), the Trustee or the caregiver is not obligated to follow your specific instructions in that trust. But if the purpose of the Pet Trust is not being fulfilled, the trust "reverts" back to the Executor or Personal Representative of your estate and he or she will have to figure out what to do with your pet.

The problem with an Honorary Trust is that it clearly has no bite. So if you live in Wisconsin, you should be sure you can trust your Executor (or Personal Representative, as it is called there) or the Trustee of the Honorary Pet Trust to carry out your wishes or you will need to consult an attorney to draft a Traditional Pet Trust, as described below.

Statutory Trust. Forty-five states and the District of Columbia have adopted statutes making Pet Trusts enforceable and the list grows longer each year. For example, Massachusetts adopted its Pet Trust law in 2011. Kentucky, Louisiana, Minnesota, Mississippi, and West Virginia do not have any laws authorizing Pet Trusts as this book goes to press.

A Statutory Pet Trust exists by mention in your Will. It is a simple plan that meets the minimal requirements under state law. It does not allow you to make as many decisions regarding the terms of the trust as you might under a Traditional Pet Trust. For example, a provision in your Will stating "I leave $5,000 to my nephew, John, in trust for the care of my cat, Abby" may be effective if your state law provides that trusts for pets are enforceable.

However, your state's statute may impose some limitations. For example, most state statutes give the court the ability to reduce the amount of caretaking funds to an amount which the court deems is reasonable for your pet.

Consult your attorney for guidance on whatever limitations your state may have on Pet Trusts. They may be in your state statute (see Appendix "A") or possibly even as a result of court cases, which you should discuss with your attorney.

Traditional Pet Trust. Even if you reside in a state without a Pet Trust statute, you are not out of luck because a "Traditional Pet Trust" can be effective in all states. Compared to a Statutory Pet Trust created in your Will, a Traditional Pet Trust is generally a revocable trust. (See the discussion in Chapter 10, "Closing Thoughts: Should I Do This Myself?" regarding whether this document should be prepared by an attorney or obtained from a documentation preparation service.) This trust is created in favor of a human beneficiary, who would be your pet's caregiver. The Trustee is required to make distributions to that beneficiary to cover the pet's expenses, provided that the beneficiary-caregiver is taking good care of your pet.

In this arrangement there are two people involved: the beneficiary-caregiver and a Trustee. However, it is also possible for the beneficiary-caregiver to be the same person as the Trustee.

This technique gives you more control than a Statutory Pet Trust as it allows you to designate what type of pet-related expenses the Trustee must pay, and the type of care your pet is to receive. It also describes what happens if the beneficiary-caregiver can no longer care for the animal, and the disposition of the pet after the pet dies (e.g., cremation or burial).

Tax on Creation of the Trust: Income, Gift or Estate Tax?

When a Pet Trust is created — and funded — the transfer of funds to the trust does not constitute income to anyone. It is not income to the Trustee or the caregiver, regardless of whether it is funded by a lifetime gift or with a bequest after death.

If the trust is funded by a lifetime gift, the transfer to the trust will constitute a gift, which could be subject to *federal gift tax*, depending on the amount of gift tax exemption the person creating the trust still has at the time of the gift, and possible exclusions. Under current law, effective in 2011 and 2012, a person can give away up to $5 million (the *federal gift tax exemption*) during his or her lifetime without actually being liable for federal gift tax, and gifts which exceed that amount are subject to 35% federal gift tax. (Be alert to future legislation which may change this amount and rate.) Further, it may be possible to avoid using any of the $5 million gift tax exemption by using the annual gift tax exclusion ($13,000 per recipient in 2011, subject to inflation adjustment in future years), if the trust is properly drafted and administered. Any gift tax would generally be the responsibility of the donor — the person making the contribution to the trust — not the Trustee or the caregiver.

If the trust is funded by a bequest on the death of the pet owner, not a lifetime gift, then there could be *federal estate tax* liability. Effective for 2011 and 2012, each person has a $5 million *federal estate tax exemption*, and estates in excess of that amount are generally subject to federal estate tax at a 35% rate. Once again, be alert to future legislation which could change this amount and rate.

The federal estate tax and the gift tax are "unified," which means that lifetime gifts which use part of the gift tax exemption will reduce the estate tax exemption available upon death. Generally the federal estate tax, if any, would be the responsibility of the estate of the decedent, i.e., the person leaving the bequest to create the Pet Trust.

If you have the foresight to set up an Irrevocable Trust during your lifetime, which is the owner of life insurance on your life, it may be possible to avoid estate tax on the life insurance proceeds. That Irrevocable Trust can be a Pet Trust, or in some cases can fund a Pet Trust.

Example 1

Assumed Facts: Ed dies in 2012 with an estate valued at $5,100,000, including $100,000 life insurance owned by Ed and payable to his estate. His wife died many years ago and he has not remarried.

He leaves $100,000 to a Pet Trust for his poodle, Charlie, and the balance of his estate ($5 million) to his children. There are no charitable bequests, and thus no charitable deductions, and let's assume that he has prepaid his funeral expenses and that there are no other expenses to administer the estate. (His son is a lawyer and handles it all at no charge.)

Results: Since his estate exceeds the $5 million estate tax exemption, there will be federal estate tax on the excess, i.e., on $100,000, which just happens to be the amount going to the Pet Trust. Under current law (in effect in 2011-2012) the rate will be 35%, so $35,000 federal estate tax will be payable. (Future legislation could change this result.) Depending on how his Will or Trust is drafted, that tax could be payable by the children. There could also be state inheritance or estate tax implications, depending on where Ed lives.

Planning Possibilities: If Ed wants the Pet Trust to get the full $100,000, then he will want to make sure that the Will or Trust allocates the tax to the children's share of the estate. Otherwise, the tax could reduce the amount going to the Pet Trust. Ed could have eliminated the estate tax by having the life insurance held in an Irrevocable Life Insurance Trust. Either the Trustee of that trust could have been made the original owner of that policy, or an existing policy could have been transferred to that trust more than three years prior to his death.

The Bottom Line: In view of the large federal gift tax and estate tax exemptions—at least under the law in effect in 2011-2012—and the amounts which are typically transferred to a Pet Trust, it is extremely unlikely that the funding of a Pet Trust will generate either gift tax or estate tax. Consult your attorney if you have questions about how the estate or gift tax could affect your situation, and be on the alert for changes in future legislation. Also, there may be *state gift or estate or inheritance taxes*, depending on your state. A discussion of these taxes is outside the scope of this book, so ask your attorney about these taxes as well.

Income Taxation:

Who Pays Tax on the Trust's Income and Distributions?

If the money in a Pet Trust generates income, the question is who pays income tax on that income. Although the answer may turn on what type of Pet Trust is involved, there are three possibilities:

1. You, as the pet owner and person who set up the trust, if you created and funded it during your lifetime;

2. The beneficiary of the trust, which is not the pet, but the person whom you have designated as the pet's caregiver; or

3. The trust itself, if it is treated by the tax law as a taxable entity.

The following are some general rules of thumb in typical situations, and points to watch out for:

First, if you set up the trust during your lifetime, and if you reserve the right to revoke it, then you will be taxable on the trust's income and the tax will be based on your adjusted gross income. The trust will be ignored for income tax purposes.

Second, if the trust is *not* revocable—either it is irrevocable on creation (i.e., drafted so it cannot be changed), or you set it up in your estate planning so it takes effect only upon your death—then either the trust itself or the human beneficiary may be taxed on the income. The human beneficiary may be the same person as your pet's caregiver.

Third, if the trust earns income which is not distributed out of the trust but is retained in the trust, then the trust itself will be taxable on that income. Tax rates applicable to trusts typically are much higher than rates applicable to individuals with the same amount of income.

However, if the irrevocable trust distributes money from the trust to the human beneficiary, in some cases the trust's income will, in effect, be carried out of the trust and taxable to that beneficiary. Thus, the beneficiary could be subject to income tax on all or part of the money received — even if the beneficiary uses that money to take care of the pet. Further, if the beneficiary receives compensation for caregiver services, that will also be subject to income tax.

Fourth, income tax treatment of Honorary and Statutory Pet Trusts, on the one hand, and Traditional Pet Trusts, on the other, may be different. While a Traditional Pet Trust has a human beneficiary, Honorary and Statutory Pet Trusts have a non-human beneficiary, i.e., your pet. If you set up an Honorary or Statutory Pet Trust, it is likely the trust will be taxed at the normal trust rates, but distributions made from the trust will not be taxable income to your pet nor will they be deductible to the trust for income tax purposes. IRS Revenue Ruling 76-486 confirms this. (Rev. Rul. 76-486, 1976-2 C.B. 192.)

With a Traditional Pet Trust that has a human beneficiary who is usually the caregiver, to the extent the trust has income he or she pays income taxes on distributions from the trust (unless the trust is set up so that you, as the creator or settlor of the trust, are taxed on it during your lifetime). And those distributions are deductible to the trust.

Ultimately, because Honorary and Statutory Pet Trusts have non-human beneficiaries, the income tax on trust income could be higher than for a Traditional Pet Trust. This is because these trusts may have to pay income tax on trust income, even if distributed, and are unable to take a deduction for those distributions. With a Traditional Pet Trust, distributions are made to a human beneficiary, taxable at his or her individual tax rate to the extent of trust income, and the trust is able to take an income tax deduction for those distributions.

A major tax advantage of a Traditional Pet Trust (which has a human beneficiary) is therefore that the trust may distribute all its income so that the income is taxable at the individual beneficiary's lower rate, compared to the trust paying taxes on those distributions at a higher tax rate applicable to trusts.

Example 2

Assumed Facts: Mike creates a Traditional Pet Trust with $100,000 for the care of his pet parrot, Lucy. He designates his brother, John, as Trustee of the trust, to watch over the money and make distributions according to the trust. He also designates his neighbor, Alice, as caregiver for Lucy, with Alice's daughter, Jennifer, as her successor if Alice can no longer serve.

John is to invest the money conservatively and give money to Alice, monthly or more often if needed, for all of the parrot's expenses. In addition, John is to give Alice $500 per year from the trust for her services. On the parrot's death, any balance in the trust is to be distributed to the local Humane Society. John, as Trustee, invests the money in a savings account and the trust earns $1,000 during the year.

During the year John distributes $1,500 to Alice, which she uses for the parrot's food, toys, other supplies, pet-sitting during Alice's vacation, and veterinary checkups. In addition, John gives Alice $500 for her caregiver services.

Result: Alice has $500 of compensation income, i.e., the amount she receives for her services as caregiver. This seems right but may not be expected. Alice may think she was going to receive a non-taxable gift. However, Alice will also be taxable on $1,000 of the trust's income which passed through to her with the $1,500 distribution, even though she used the distribution to pay for the parrot's expenses. Assuming that Alice is taxable at a combined state and federal tax rate of 30%, she will have to pay $300 income tax on that distribution, in addition to the tax on her $500 compensation income from the trust.

Planning Possibilities: First, how can this income tax burden on part of the $1,500 distribution Alice used for the parrot's care be avoided? If the trust does not earn taxable income, then there will be no taxable income which could pass through to the beneficiary. For example, if all the trust's assets are invested in a non-interest bearing checking account, or other non-income producing assets (e.g., appreciating stock with no dividends), the trust would not generate any income.

Second, if the trust pays the parrot's expenses directly and doesn't distribute the amount for the expenses to the beneficiary, then the trust will be taxable on all its income. This can avoid the income tax for the beneficiary, but could result in more taxes being paid overall because the trust's income tax rates could be higher than the individual beneficiary's rate.

Could the trust provide that the trust will also pay the beneficiary an amount equal to the beneficiary's income tax associated with distributions from the trust? Probably so, but this payment will then create additional taxable income to the beneficiary, which will generate more income tax. If the trust then pays that additional tax, that will create additional income, and yet more tax will be created, until the additional income by paying the tax on the tax becomes negligible and is zeroed out. Implications of paying the caregiver's income taxes should thus be carefully considered and, if this outcome is really intended, it should be covered in careful drafting of the trust.

Future legislation could change the income taxation of Pet Trusts by providing an income tax deduction for pet care expenses. In 2009, Rep. Thaddeus McCotter (R-Mich) introduced a bill in Congress, the Humanity and Pets Partnered Through the Years (or "HAPPY") Act, H.R. 3501, which would allow an individual who legally owns a pet an income deduction for qualified pet care expenses, not to exceed $3,500 per year. That bill was referred to the House Ways and Means Committee.

The amounts would have to be paid during the year for qualified pet care expenses, so a contribution to a trust for future payment of pet care expenses would not fall within the scope of the deduction. Also, since the law provides for a deduction for individuals, changes would be needed to permit a Pet Trust to take the deduction.

Further, it provides that the pet must be legally owned by the person taking the deduction, so ownership of the pet would have to tie in with payment of the expenses. In other words, if the Pet Trust owns the pet, the trust (not the caregiver) would have to pay the pet care expenses. Clearly some changes would be needed if that law was to be applicable to payments made by Pet Trusts.

What about the payment for the caregiver-beneficiary's services? Compensation income is generally taxable. However, if Mike's Will or Revocable Trust had provided for a *bequest* to the caregiver rather than compensation, it is possible that it would have been treated as a bequest—which is not taxable income—and the services would have been provided without compensation. Obviously prepayment carries risks, e.g., that the person receiving the bequest may not perform the services, or would have no incentive to perform them well, or might die before the pet dies, possibly even right after having received the money. Also, if the pet dies earlier than anticipated, the caregiver will have been paid for services not rendered, and less will pass to the remainder beneficiary, the Humane Society in this case.

Are Charitable Deductions Available?

If you are concerned about estate tax liability, i.e., if your estate is larger than $5 million (or $10 million for married couples) or if Congress reduces this exemption amount significantly, a testamentary "Charitable Remainder Trust" is one technique that you might consider. By creating a charitable estate tax deduction, you could benefit your heirs and your favorite charity.

In this type of a trust, a beneficiary receives distributions of income during his or her life or for a specific term of years. On the beneficiary's death (or when the term expires), whatever is left (the "remainder") goes to the specified charity. Your estate gets an estate tax deduction for the value of the remainder interest which will pass to the charity in the future, after the beneficiary's interest terminates (assuming all tax requirements are met). The remainder interest is computed on an actuarial basis, since we don't know when the trust is created exactly how much will ultimately pass to the charity.

Can you tie this technique with a Pet Trust? Not if your pet is the beneficiary. Not yet, at least. The IRS has specifically held in Revenue Ruling 78-105 that amounts passing to a Pet Trust for the lifetime benefit of a pet with the remainder to charity does not qualify for the charitable estate tax deduction. (Rev. Rul. 78-105, 1978-1 C.B. 295.) The reason is that a pet is not a "person." In that ruling, the Trustee was directed to make monthly distributions of a fixed amount for pet's care. The Internal Revenue Code requires distributions from a Charitable Remainder Trust be made payable to or for the use of a person or persons. Similarly, if the trust is set up during your lifetime, no charitable income tax deduction would be allowed on funding this trust even if the remainder interest is reserved for a charity.

However, this could change someday. In 2001, Rep. Earl Blumenauer (D-OR) introduced a bill, the Charitable Remainder Pet Trust Act, H.R. 1796 (otherwise known as the "Morgan Bill," named after his pet collie, Morgan), to amend the Internal Revenue Code to treat Charitable Remainder Pet Trusts in a manner similar to other Charitable Remainder Annuity Trusts. The bill went to the House Ways and Means Committee but was not acted upon. It was reintroduced in 2007, as H.R. 2941, and was referred to the Ways and Means Committee.

In the meantime, you could still set up a Charitable Remainder Trust with your pet's caregiver (rather than your pet) as the current beneficiary, with the remainder going to charity. This will give the caregiver an income stream for life, or for a term of years. Estate and income tax deductions would be available for the value of the remainder interest passing to the charity. If this seems of interest to you, discuss it with an attorney who is familiar with Charitable Remainder Trusts and planning for pets.

Among other things, you should realize that if you set up a Charitable Remainder Trust for the caregiver's lifetime, that could be longer than your pet's life expectancy. If you set up a Charitable Remainder Trust for a term of years, you may want to base that term on your pet's life expectancy, but at what point should the pet's life expectancy be determined? If you decide on the term of years when you draft the trust, the life expectancy will be longer at that point in time than it will be when the trust ultimately is funded and goes into full effect at your death. 🐾

"Most pets display so many human-like traits
and emotions it's easy to forget they're not
gifted with the English language and then
get snubbed when we talk to them
and they don't say anything back."

— Stephenie Geist

Chapter 8
LOSS OF A PET OWNER OR A PET:
GRIEF SUPPORT

In this chapter we will address two related topics: First, what will your pet go through if something happens to you? Since this is a book on your planning for your pet's welfare in the event of your disability or death, this is a logical area of concern. It's also something of which the person you appoint as caregiver should be made aware.

Second, as you consider your own planning, how will you deal with the loss of a pet? We are interested in planning for both the case when your pet has to live without you, and the possibility that you have to endure the loss of a pet.

Do Pets Grieve?

While generalizations should be avoided, and it will certainly depend on the type of pet, it is clear that many pets will grieve the loss of an owner.

There are endless stories of pets suffering the loss of their human companions, and each day brings a new story.

As this book was in its final drafting stage, we saw gut wrenching photos on the Internet of a dog lying alone at his owner's grave in Brazil, where he has been for days. The photos show a mixed breed in a lonely vigil next to a cross of unpainted wood stuck into pile of red dirt. The horrific flooding in Brazil and mud slides rocked the country and the world, claiming hundreds of lives. But in addition to the tremendous personal toll, which numbed the country and the world by the enormity of the catastrophe, this photo was a poignant reminder of the losses that pets suffer when their owners are taken away from them.

The ways in which pets can respond to feelings of grief are highly varied, but changes in normal behavior are not unusual. Signs the pet is reacting to a loss may be noticeable, such as the dog refusing to leave his owner's graveside, or more subtle.

Pets may lose interest in eating and even refuse to eat. They may constantly whine or isolate themselves, losing interest in cuddling. One dog wandered around the house for hours, searching for her master after he died, but couldn't find him. The dog knew that a change in the family structure had taken place, but couldn't understand it. Another hid himself away in the furnace room in the basement, and slept for hours.

One cat fell into deep depression after the death of her elderly companion. She needed months of medical care, including force feeding, to save her life.

A dog waited at the school bus stop each day for his owner, who had died and would never come home from school again.

It is not unusual to hear of dogs or cats who cry out, sit at the window or gate for hours waiting for the return of their lost owner, lose their appetite, are unable to sleep, become lethargic, seem fatigued, are withdrawn (or become more clingy), and lose interest in their favorite activities.

One woman reported that after her father died, his poodle plopped himself down in her dad's easy chair and wouldn't get out except for brief meals and to relieve herself. She lost her appetite, refused to play, and wouldn't sit with anyone else. It took her several months to get over the loss of her best friend.

Some pets may react badly when left alone in the house, scratching the door, although this was never an issue before.

The loss of someone can cause stress for a pet, and that stress can show itself in various ways, such as stomach upsets, hair loss, or inappropriate excreting behavior.

Why do we mention this in a book on estate planning for pet owners? Because both you and the person you select as your pet's caregiver should be aware of the loss your pet may feel if something happens to you. This should be an additional motivating factor to encourage you to do proper planning, and your caregiver should be made aware that things will not necessarily be as they were when you were around. Frankly, it could be a difficult and painful time, not only for your family, if you have one, but also for your pet and for your pet's caregiver.

How should the pet's caregiver handle this situation? Patience and love will help, but may not be sufficient. Professional help from a veterinarian who understands pet grief can help both the pet and the caregiver. The vet can provide insight and recommend an individualized course of action, depending on the type of pet and the kind of behavior which is being shown. Medication may be involved in some cases. You should be aware of this potential additional medical expense in considering how much is enough to fund your pet's care.

For dogs and cats, some say that the grieving process can take a couple of weeks, but in some cases signs of depression and anxiety have lasted for six months or more.

What should the caregiver do during this difficult time for the pets? Aside from going to the vet and following the vet's advice, the caregiver may want to show the pets extra special attention. Go for walks, play with them, especially their favorite games. Create some "quality time" with the pets. But don't overdo it because a subsquent cut back could result in separation anxiety.

Also be aware that the way your family is reacting to the loss may affect your pets, who will be sensitive to what is going on around them. Your caregiver should be aware of this in reacting to the pets' behavior. The place may be more noisy or frenetic than usual. There may be more people around, and the people may be new to the pets. The pets may pick up on whether the people are upbeat or depressed, or whether they are snapping at each other and bickering.

The pets may be like a canary in a coal mine, an early warning signal that there are issues that have to be dealt with in the family. Misbehavior on the part of the pets may be an indicator that there are issues with the family's overall emotional health and how the family is dealing with the loss, which are separate yet related issues to be dealt with.

Grieving the Loss of a Pet

When we consider estate planning for a pet owner, we also think about what might happen in the event the pet owner loses the pet. In some cases, this loss and the grief that follows will be much like grieving any other beloved member of your family—with perhaps one major difference:

Sometimes people will just not understand your deep loss. Without intending to hurt you or diminish your feelings, they may say things such as "Just get over it. It's only an animal. Go get yourself another one."

Comments of this type may not be intended to be cruel and uncaring. They just do not understand your pain. Don't let anyone tell you that it's silly or overly sentimental to feel the way you do. Give yourself permission to grieve. Only you know what you are feeling. The death of a pet is the loss of a nonjudgmental love source. You have lost a friend, someone you nurtured and cared for.

Grieving the loss of a pet can involve the same stages of grief as grieving the death of a person. You may not experience them all, or they may not be in the same order. They include denial, anger, guilt, depression, acceptance, and resolution. The fact that the loved one was a pet and that you were the pet's owner and arguably had more control over life and death decisions may influence how some of these stages of grief will play themselves out. Nonetheless, your grief will be real, and may even seem overwhelming at times.

You may be in denial and refuse to accept the fact that your pet has died or that death is unavoidable. This could begin as early as when your first learn that the animal's illness or injuries are life-threatening. If death is sudden, the loss may be especially hard to accept and the urge to deny it may be stronger.

Denial is often followed by anger. People you normally love and respect may be the object of your anger. They may include your family, your friends, and even your veterinarian. You may blame your veterinarian for not doing more to save your pet. You may say things you don't really mean. You may blame family members for not encouraging you to spend more on treatment, for urging you to "let it go." If your pet was entrusted to someone else, you may blame that person for being careless and allowing whatever happened to happen.

You may be plagued by guilt. You may ask yourself if you did the right thing, if you did enough, or too much. Regardless of how and when your pet dies, you may have some of these thoughts and blame yourself. Even though you feel responsible for your pet, you should not automatically jump to the conclusion that you failed to protect your pet because you lost the pet.

You may show signs of depression. This will be no less real because you have suffered the loss of a pet. You may find yourself crying uncontrollably, and you may be totally drained of all your energy. You may refuse to socialize, literally locking yourself up, away from friends and family. You may not be able to pull yourself out of bed in the morning, and this may be even more common if your morning routine involved feeding your pet or taking your pet for a walk. It may literally be impossible for you to do daily tasks which you could have easily done before the loss.

You may even find yourself asking if you can continue to live without your pet. While you may need some special assistance to get through this stage, you can do it. If you experience deep depression, you should seek professional assistance. With time, you will be able to come to terms with your loss and accept your pet's death. You will be able to remember your pet and your time together without the intense grief and emotional pain that you felt at the time of the loss. It will no longer feel like someone has ripped your heart out. You will still feel a sense of loss, but the fact that you have accepted it will mean that you have come to terms with the fact that your pet has died. At some point the feelings of anger, guilt and depression will be replaced by fond memories.

The hardest thing may be to deal with family and friends who just don't understand what you are going through. However, if you understand that your reactions are normal, it will help you cope with your feelings and deal with the feelings of others around you. They need to understand that sorrow and grief are normal and natural responses to the loss of a loved one, human or animal. Be honest with yourself and others about how you feel.

If you are really having a difficult time and in despair, if your grief is overtaking you, seek out someone who will listen to you about how you feel about the loss of your pet. Your veterinarian certainly understands the depth of the relationship and may be able to suggest support groups and hot lines, grief counselors, clergymen, social workers, physicians, or psychologists who can help. This way you may be able to get the support you need to cope with your loss. Your Humane Society may also be able to direct you, and numerous support groups can be found through the Internet. (Some of these resources are listed at the end of this chapter.)

Some people turn inward, while others find it helpful to express their feelings outwardly. They write down their memories in poems or stories, or put together photo books. Some use pet bereavement chat rooms on the Internet to meet with other pet owners who have suffered a loss. This helps them realize that their feelings are normal, and see how others have dealt with them. Others rearrange their schedules to fill the time periods each day which would previously have been spent with their pet.

Don't be afraid to look for help, and don't be ashamed to talk about your sorrow. But remember also to talk about the good times, the fun that you and your pet had together, the things you liked to do and enjoyed together, and the good memories.

The grief of a pet owner on the loss of a beloved pet is probably the most frustrating and emotional experience one can have. This is due in large part to the fact that our society in general doesn't recognize the grief of a pet owner. As a result, pet owners often feel marginalized and isolated. Today more resources than ever before exist to help bereaved pet owners realize that what they are feeling is entirely normal, and part of life's journey.

Should You Get Another Animal?

A common question raised by someone who loses a pet is whether they should get another animal. There is no single answer which will apply in every case.

Some people feel that they would never want to go through such a loss again. Therefore, they feel they would never want another animal. The mere thought of having, and at some point losing, another animal seems unbearable.

One of our clients had to leave Austria in World War II, during the Nazi occupation. Her escape was to Shanghai, China, which she would reach in a 4-month journey by train through Poland, Russia, Siberia, and Manchuria, with outside temperatures down to 45 degrees below zero. That portion of the trip alone was over 5,000 miles, in conditions so hard she could never bring herself to talk about them even decades later.

Before she left Austria she took her cats and a dog, a 13 year-old shiatsu, to a veterinarian, and had them euthanized so they would not suffer. Although she remained an animal lover, she could never have another pet, because she constantly remembered the pain she suffered from the loss of her dog and cats. She lived with those memories the rest of her life, over 60 years, to age 97, and never had another pet of any kind. In her estate plan she left 50% of her estate to the Humane Society, a firm acknowledgment of the love she felt for her pets.

For some people, like that client, these feelings may never pass. For others, they will pass over time. For others, a new animal may help them recover from their loss more quickly. But rushing that decision before you are really ready — or insisting that a family member get another pet because you feel it would be a good thing — may make the person feel that the grief is not real and can be resolved by just getting another animal.

The decision as to whether and when to bring a new pet into your life is an intensely personal one. Making that decision before the grief is resolved may only compound the grief. The right message may be that although the animal who has died cannot be replaced, it may be possible to find another pet to share your life. You will be ready to do that when you are no longer looking back and mourning your loss, but are ready to move forward and create a new relationship.

On the following page we provide a few of the many, many resources on pet loss grief support.

Additional Resources: Pet Loss Grief Support

The ASPCA (American Society for the Prevention of Cruelty to Animals) maintains a Pet Loss Support and Bereavement Counseling Hotline, (877) 474-3310. Their website also provides links to other organizations which address pet loss. http://www.aspca.org/about-us/faq/pet-death.aspx

The Pet Loss Support Page has links to support groups and counselors throughout the country, state by state, in connection with loss of a pet. http://www.pet-loss.net

The Association for Pet Loss and Bereavement has links to many resources, including an extensive bibliography. http://aplb.org/index.html

Michigan State University College of Veterinary Medicine maintains a Pet Loss Support Hotline, (517) 432-2696. http://www.cvm.msu.edu/petloss

University of Illinois College of Veterinary Medicine also maintains a Companion Animal Related Emotions (C.A.R.E.) Pet Loss Helpline, (877) 394-CARE (2273). http://www.vetmed.illinois.edu/CARE/

Cornell University College of Veterinary Medicine maintains a Pet Loss Support Hotline, (607) 253-3932, and has links to other resources, including other hotlines, on its website. http://www.vet.cornell.edu/org/petloss/

Telephone hotlines often have limited hours, so please check the website for their hours of staffing.

These websites represent but a tiny fraction of the Internet resources on pet loss grief support. We have no mechanism for judging or verifying the competence of the individuals or organizations mentioned on these websites. Therefore, we are not recommending or endorsing any of the above or the sources mentioned on these websites, but are merely providing them for our readers' information. ❧

"The difference between friends and pets
is that friends we allow into our company,
pets we allow into our solitude."

– *Robert Brault*

Chapter 9
MEMORIALIZE YOUR PET;
LEAVE A LEGACY

There are countless ways to remember your pet, and for you to leave your own legacy in terms of support for animal causes, animal rights, animal rescue, education for pet owners and the like. Most of us don't know if we will survive our pet, or if our pet will survive us. We therefore suggest you plan for both possibilities, and consider also the broader good you can do for animal causes in general, by taking the opportunity in your estate planning to benefit a charitable organization which benefits animals. First, however, let's briefly address the possibility that you will survive your pet.

Memorializing Your Pet: Dealing with Pet Remains

When a pet dies, you must choose how to handle its remains. Sometimes, in the midst of grief, it may seem easiest to leave the pet at the clinic for disposal. Check with your clinic to find out whether there is a fee for such disposal. Some shelters also accept such remains, though many charge a fee for disposal.

If you prefer a more formal option, several are available. Home burial is a popular choice, if you have sufficient property for it. It is economical and enables you to design your own funeral ceremony at little cost. However, city regulations usually prohibit pet burials, and this is not a good choice for renters or people who move frequently. Typically, home burial is permitted in rural and suburban settings only. A tight-fitting wooden box will help safeguard the animal's remains.

To many, a pet cemetery provides a sense of dignity, security, and permanence. Owners appreciate the serene surroundings and care of the grave site. Cemetery costs vary depending on the services you select, as well as upon the type of pet you have. The costs for cemetery burial vary, from around $200 for a simple burial to thousands of dollars for elaborate services. Many pet cemeteries will cooperate with veterinary clinics, sending a representative to handle details.

Communal burial is a less costly option that is offered by many pet cemeteries and private humane organizations. Your companion animal's dignity is in no way affected by burial with other animals. Communal burial is a common choice.

Cremation is a less expensive option that allows you to handle your pet's remains in a variety of ways: bury them (even in the city), scatter them in a favorite location, place them in a columbarium, or even keep them with you in a decorative urn, which are available in many styles and at a wide range of prices.

In areas where land is expensive, communal cremation is a sensible alternative. Some veterinary clinics even have their own crematories, as do many pet cemeteries and humane organizations. The fee is relatively modest, often less than $100.

Your veterinarian probably can arrange for individual cremation and advise you on environmental concerns over disposal of ashes. This option is more costly than communal cremation, with fees commonly ranging from $75 to $250.

Check with your veterinarian, pet shop, or phone directory for options available in your area. Consider your living situation, personal and religious values, finances, and future plans when making your decision. It's also wise to make such plans in advance, rather than hurriedly in the midst of grief.

Memorializing Your Pet: Bringing Back Fond Memories

It is difficult to put into one category the many ways that pet owners have found to memorialize their pets, from memorial services to tangible items. The possibilities are endless, but here are a few examples, in no particular order:

1.   Hold a memorial service. Let yourself and others who knew and loved your pet say goodbye and share memories during a memorial service. You can hold a service anywhere that feels right to you — at a pet cemetery, in your backyard, in your pet's favorite park, or at any place that reminds you of special times shared with your pet.

2.   Create a living memorial. Plant trees or flowers in memory of your pet. Some people like the idea of forget-me-nots in a memorial garden, maybe with a plaque in the pet's honor. Put a special marker, like a statue, bird bath, stone lantern or customized memorial stone in the garden.

3.   Put a picture of the animal somewhere special in the house. It can be a photo from your collection, or a custom portrait. There are many pet portrait artists who can do a portrait of your pet from a favorite photo. Sculpture artists even can make a sculpture as a memorial to your pet.

4.   Create a scrapbook, photo collage, or a personalized photo book that reflects the pet's significance in your life.

5.   Journal your best memories of your pet in a poem or story. You can even incorporate this into a personalized photo book. If children are involved, they can be the illustrators, or even write part of it.

6.   Set aside a day a year as Remembrance Day.

7.   Purchase a photo key chain and place a photo of your pet in it.

8.   Have a custom flag made, including a photo or likeness of your pet, and hang it in the front of your house.

9.   Prepare a personalized photo calendar of you and your pet.

10. If your pet has been cremated, find a special place for your pet's ashes. Keep your pet's ashes in a beautiful urn or bury them in a meaningful place on your property.

11. Create an online pet memorial. You can post a photo and a story about your pet.

12. Some pet owners even take the bodies of their deceased animals to a taxidermist in order to have a statuette produced from the animal's corpse.

Leave a Legacy

Whether you survive your pet, or your pet survives you, you may also wish to make a memorial contribution to a charity in honor of your animal and the deep bond you shared. There are many worthy animal-related causes that could use your financial support. Your local or state Humane Society, animal rescue organizations, guide dog organization, and schools of veterinary medicine are among the possibilities.

Humane organizations desperately need financial support to care for homeless animals, and guide dog organizations also need support to make people's lives better. Many veterinary schools accept scholarship funds in the name of the animal or donor. ❦

"Animals are such
agreeable friends.
They ask no questions,
they pass no criticism."

— George Elliot

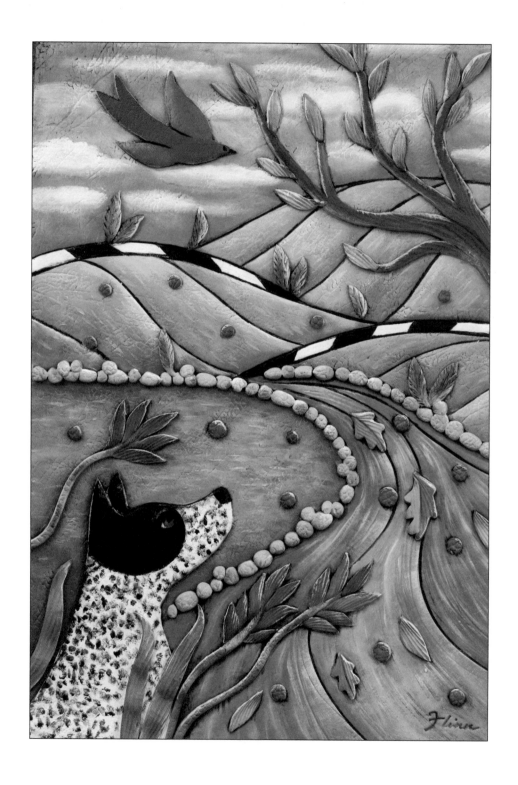

Chapter 10
CLOSING THOUGHTS:
HOW DO YOU IMPLEMENT THE PLAN?

If you have decided that you ought to plan for your pet's care and welfare should something happen to you, the next question is how do you do it? You could certainly take the informal route and just talk with the person you intend to be your pet's caregiver, and perhaps provide some amount of funding. Leaving the pet to that person in your Will, along with a bequest of cash, could also be considered.

These approaches, along with the Honorary Pet Trust and the Statutory Pet Trust, all suffer from several disadvantages which have been discussed in Chapter 6. Among other things, they may not include the level of detail that is possible in a Traditional Pet Trust. If the arrangement is in a Will, there may be delays in implementing the plan after your death because of the probate process. Also, it will not be effective in the event of your prolonged absence or disability.

We therefore recommend the Traditional Pet Trust, accompanied by a detailed Pet Information Sheet for each pet. See Appendix "D" for a sample Pet Information Sheet, which you may freely use and modify.

The Pet Trust can be drafted by an attorney experienced in planning for pets, or obtained online through a number of sources. Although we tend to favor the custom drafted document, drafted by an attorney who specializes in this area of the law after a one-on-one consultation, we recognize that some pet owners may not have the resources to go to an attorney, or there might not be a qualified attorney in your area.

We have not reviewed the trust documents generated by the online services, and cannot comment on the quality of the trust documents that they provide. In some cases, they will suggest generating their form online and then having a consultation with an estate planning attorney to make sure the document complies with your state's law and is appropriate for your overall plan.

One might ask whether it would be just as simple to go directly to the attorney, although it is conceivable that having an attorney review a draft document generated by an online program could be less costly than having the attorney draft the document. In our experience, however, reviewing a document prepared by someone else generally takes more time, and is thus more costly, than using our own document from the outset.

However, use of the online services *instead of* (not in addition to) working with an estate planning attorney experienced in planning for pet owners raises the following questions:

1. Do you feel that you can answer all the questions in our Pet Trust Drafting Checklist (Appendix "E") on your own, or do you feel you might benefit from discussion with a professional who can guide you through the options and the implications?

2. Are you comfortable with your choices as to the (a) amount of funding, (b) timing of funding (during lifetime or at your death), and (c) sources of funding? Does the online drafting program address these issues in any meaningful way, or merely ask you for the answers? Do you feel you could benefit from discussing them with an attorney?

3. Would you benefit from discussion about whether the amount you are considering is too high, and might be reduced by a court, or too low to generate sufficient cash flow for the likely term of the trust? Does the online drafting input form simply ask you for the amount you want to put in the trust without considering these potential issues?

4. Are you comfortable with your choice of caregiver for your pets, and successor caregivers? Sometimes there are issues that come up only after reflection and discussion. The problem may not be with the person you select but with their spouse or partner, other family members or roommates. Sometimes they may be a beneficiary under your main estate plan, and you may have concerns about their ability to manage their own finances, and yet you might be inclined to let them take care of your pet. Is there an inconsistency here? Would you benefit from discussion on how to split the role of caregiver and Trustee over the funds in the trust? Does the online drafting program simply ask you who you want to appoint and who would be the successor?

5.   How does the online program deal with care instructions? Are you essentially getting a Statutory Pet Trust, legally binding but not fully developed as concerns care instructions, or a fully thought out Traditional Pet Trust tailored to your specific situation?

6.   Do you know who will receive whatever is left in the trust after it terminates? Would you benefit from discussion as to possible charitable organizations, perhaps related to animal causes? Does the online program simply ask you who you want? Does it provide for successors in the event the first remainder beneficiary is no longer alive (if it is an individual) or no longer in existence (if it is a charitable organization)? Would you benefit from discussion about potential scholarship funding at a college of veterinary medicine, with whatever may be left at the termination of the trust?

7.   If you use an online program to draft a Pet Trust, how will that integrate into your overall estate plan? Would it make more sense for the Pet Trust to be part of a revocable trust plan, so that your Successor Trustee can take whatever steps are necessary to fund the Pet Trust in the event of your disability, prolonged absence, disappearance or death?

8.   Does the document generated by the online program protect against challenges by the remainder beneficiary? Although it may not be possible to eliminate challenges, certain language can reduce the risk of a successful challenge.

9.   Does your main estate plan address possible challenges of the Pet Trust by beneficiaries in the main plan who may not approve of what you are doing in the Pet Trust? Sometimes a forfeiture clause can be included to discourage unfounded challenges. If the online drafting program is only used for your Pet Trust, how would you even consider a forfeiture clause? If you decide you want such a clause, what steps should you take to make it effective under your state's law? An attorney can discuss your specific intent with you and your feelings toward the other beneficiaries. Language in the trust which fully reflects your relationship with your pet and your objectives can help a court in interpreting the trust and implementing your intentions. A consultation with an attorney can help you explore all these issues.

10. Do you have a sufficient understanding of the tax implications associated with the creation, funding and operation of the Pet Trust? How does the online program deal with tax issues? An experienced estate planning attorney with background in Pet Trusts can help you through what might otherwise be a very confusing area, and assure that you minimize adverse tax consequences and surprises for your caregiver and Trustee.

11. Is the online documentation service merely providing you a form, or providing you legal services? Read the fine print in the General Conditions or Terms of Agreement. Do they represent that the document will actually comply with the law of your state and will be appropriate for your situation? Do they provide any warranty at all or guaranty as to the Pet Trust being generated for you? Is their liability limited, in any event, to the amount paid for the document? By comparison, if you work with an attorney he or she will be fully responsible for the appropriateness of the advice and the documents prepared, or will be liable to you or your estate for damages in malpractice.

A Pet Trust drafted through some of the online programs may be better than no Pet Trust at all. However, as you can see from the above questions, in some cases a pet owner may be able to derive greater benefit and peace of mind from consultation with an attorney experienced in Pet Trusts. You will also have the assurance that the documents will do what you intend them to do.

What Will It Cost?

The costs to implement a Traditional Pet Trust with an attorney will depend on several factors, which include the following:

1. **Complexity of the Arrangement.** Will you have a relatively simple arrangement described in five or six pages, or one with much more detail involving checks and balances, such as the ability of someone to remove your caregiver (perhaps vested in a Trust Protector or group of Trust Protectors)? Will you provide for specific rules for your caregiver, or are you willing to give your caregiver broad authority and discretion?

If you are leaving your pet to a pet sanctuary, or other organization, do they have specific rules to which you must adhere? Will you be contacting various organizations, and doing "due diligence" on them, or will you need your attorney's assistance?

Sometimes organizations will provide guidelines for the documents, or they may insist that you use their documents, which your attorney should review. Will they accept documents drafted by your attorney?

If you contemplate a very high amount of funding, you can expect the fees to be higher, partly because the arrangement will likely be more complex to deal with large sums. On the other hand, if you contemplate fairly nominal funding, you don't want to spend a fortune to get the legal work done, even though your pet's care is priceless. You will need to find a reasonably priced legal solution, or an attorney with compassion who will do whatever is required to help you put a plan in place which is feasible in view of your budget.

2. **The Attorney's Background.** The attorney's credentials and experience in trust law are likely to affect the attorney's normal hourly rates. However, that does not mean that the attorney will charge more than an inexperienced attorney for a Pet Trust.

If it's the first time the attorney is drafting a Pet Trust, the attorney will need to do considerable research to get up to speed, and the attorney may or may not be willing to write off some of that start-up time. More experience in estate planning for pet owners may actually allow the attorney to be more efficient and charge less. This is because the attorney will be more familiar with the issues and possible solutions. Greater efficiency should keep the costs down.

You may already work with an estate planning attorney but he or she may have no experience with Pet Trusts. This is often the case since estate planning for pet owners is a sub-specialty in estate planning. In that event, ask your attorney if he or she would be willing to consult with an attorney who has that experience, to help both of you implement the plan.

3. **Geographical Locaton**. Attorney fees tend to vary based on geographical location, as do office rents, salries for staff, and other costs of providing legal services. However, fees of attorneys in small towns are not necessarily lower than fees of attorneys in large cities, and fees can vary widely for what appears to be the same service. Don't hesitate to ask whether fees will be hourly and, if so, what the rate will be, or whether a fixed fee arrangement is available.

4. **Integration with Your Main Estate Plan**. Do you already have your estate plan in place, or do you need a review of your plan or a brand new plan into which the Pet Trust should be integrated? Is the amount you intend to leave to your Pet Trust so large that you can expect challenges from other beneficiaries—or "would-be" beneficiaries of your estate—which should be considered in drafting your documents?

5. **Pre-Meeting Preparation.** How much thought have you given to the details before meeting with your attorney? One major benefit of "doing your homework" by reading this book and completing the drafting checklist, to the extent you can, is that you will be aware of the issues, and will have resolved many of them yourself before you meet with your attorney. The more you can decide before you meet, the faster the process should go, and that should keep the costs down. Are you still struggling with some of the decisions? If so, an attorney may help you make some decisions, but this will probably take a little more time than a plan in which all the decisions are made and the document only needs to be drafted.

If you have the attorney do your basic estate planning at the same time, the time in consultation can benefit the entire process, and the additional time to draft the Pet Trust may be minimal. Though it is often difficult to determine legal fees in advance, feel free to ask any attorney you are considering whether he or she has experience with Pet Trusts, and approximately how much they typically cost.

The Last Word

By reading this book you have taken an important step in the right direction. Next, you should complete the Pet Information Sheet (Appendix "D"), which will be useful no matter what type of arrangement you decide to implement. If you feel a Traditional Pet Trust is right for you, complete the Pet Trust Drafting Checklist (Appendix "E"), then schedule an appointment with an attorney to discuss next steps. Even if this merely represents your preliminary thoughts on the essential questions, it will help you focus on the issues and facilitate further discussion and drafting of the documents. 🐾

STATE STATUTES RELATING TO

WILL AND TRUST PROVISIONS ON PET TRUSTS

Under the law of trusts prior to specific legislation, a pet owner had limited ability to create a legally binding trust for the benefit of his or her pets, to assure that the animals would be taken care of after the pet owner's death. Attempts to create trusts for this purpose faced a major obstacle: A trust needed a beneficiary, and a pet didn't qualify because a pet animal was considered personal property. Only human beings could be beneficiaries of a trust.

In 1990 the National Conference of Commissioners on Uniform State Laws ("NCCUSL") adopted the Uniform Probate Code ("UPC"), which paved the way for states to adopt specific laws on pet trusts. It included a provision which allowed for a trust for the care of a pet which outlives its owner. UPC Section 2-907(b) provided for enforceable trusts for the care of a designated domestic animal and the animal's offspring. Later, in 2000, NCCUSL adopted the Uniform Trust Code, Section 408 of which updated the prior provision by referring to a trust for any animal, not just a pet, and authorizing persons with an interest in the welfare of the animal to petition the court for appointment or removal of an enforcer of the trust.

Uniform Laws, such as the UPC and the UTC, are not laws. They are considered by state legislatures, which may or may not adopt them, and may change them prior to adoption. Therefore, it is important to review the relevant state statute to see whether and to what extent it conforms to the uniform law. However, the NCCUSL commentary on the uniform law may be helpful in interpreting the state statute. The full texts of the UPC and UTC, as well as comments on the relevant provisions, are available at the NCCUSL website, www.nccusl.org.

As of 2011, 45 states and the District of Columbia have adopted one of these model law provisions, or their own version of animal trust legislation. Only Kentucky, Louisiana, Minnesota, Mississippi and West Virginia have no statute dealing with pet trusts. However, a Traditional Pet Trust can be done in any state.

The following table of state statutes relating to pet trusts was provided by the Animal Legal & Historical Center of Michigan State University College of Law, www.animallaw.info, and is used with permission. It has been slightly modified to include references to the UPC and UTC, and updated to reflect current developments at the time of printing.

Laws can be repealed or amended. Consult your attorney to assure that your planning is based on the current law in effect in your state and to determine how the law applies in your case. Note from the effective dates the recent enactment of many of these laws; however, in some cases there were prior statutes which were superseded by the current statute.

State	Citation	Summary
Alabama Trust for care of animal	AL ST § 19-3B-110; AL ST § 19-3B-408 (based on UTC § 408) Eff. 1/1/2007	This Alabama statute provides that a trust may be created to provide for the care of an animal alive during the settlor's lifetime. The trust terminates upon the death of the animal or, if the trust was created to provide for the care of more than one animal alive during the settlor's lifetime, upon the death of the last surviving animal.
Alaska Honorary trusts; trusts for pets	AK ST § 13.12.907 (based on UPC § 2-907) Eff. 1996	This Alaska statute provides that trusts for the continuing care of designated domestic animals are valid, provided they are a duration of 21 years or less. The trust terminates when a living animal is no longer covered by the trust. Any remaining trust funds do not go to the trustee, but rather transfer by the order stipulated in the statute.
Arizona Honorary trusts; trusts for pets; condition	AZ ST § 14-2907; AZ ST § 14-10408 (based on UPC § 2-907) Eff. 1/1/1995; amended 7/10/2009	This Arizona statute provides that a trust may be created to provide for the care of an animal alive during the settlor's lifetime. The trust terminates upon the death of the animal or, if the trust was created to provide for the care of more than one animal alive during the settlor's lifetime, upon the death of the last surviving animal.
Arkansas Trusts - Trust for care of animal	AR ST § 28-73-408 (based on UTC § 408) Eff. 9/1/2005	This Arkansas statute provides that a trust may be created to provide for the care of an animal alive during the settlor's lifetime. The trust terminates upon the death of the animal or, if the trust was created to provide for the care of more than one animal alive during the settlor's lifetime, upon the death of the last surviving animal.
California Trusts - Trusts for care of animals; duration	CA PROBATE § 15212 Eff. 1/1/2009	This California statute provides that a person can create a trust for the care of a designated domestic or pet animal for the life of the animal. The duration will only be for the life of the pet, even if the trust instrument contemplates a longer duration. Note that the statute uses the singular form of "animal" and the term "domestic" or "pet" is used.

State	Citation	Summary
Colorado Trusts - Honorary trusts; trusts	CO ST § 15-11-901 (based on UPC § 2-907) Eff. 1/1/1995	This Colorado statute provides that trust for the care of designated domestic or pet animals and the animals' offspring in gestation is valid. The determination of the "animals' offspring in gestation" is made at the time the designated domestic or pet animals become present beneficiaries of the trust. Unless the trust instrument provides for an earlier termination, the trust terminates when no living animal is covered by the trust (but no longer than 21 years). The trust property then transfers as provided by statute, but the trustee may not convert the trust property.
Connecticut Trust to provide for care of animal: Creation. Administration. Jurisdiction. Termination	CT ST § 45a-489a Eff. 1/1/2009	This Connecticut statute provides that a testamentary or inter vivos trust may be created to provide for the care of an animal or animals alive during the settlor's or testator's lifetime. The trust terminates when the last surviving animal named in the trust dies. The trust must designate a "trust protector" who acts on behalf of the animals named in the trust.
Delaware Trust - Trust for care of an animal	DE ST TI 12 § 3555 Eff. 8/1/2008	This Delaware statute provides that a trust for the care of one or more specific animals living at the settlor's death is valid. The trust terminates upon the death of all animals living at the settlor's death and covered by the terms of the trust.
District of Columbia Trusts - Trust for care of animal	DC ST § 19-1304.08 (based on UTC § 408) Eff. 3/10/2004	This statute represents the District of Columbia's pet trust law. The law provides that a trust may be created to provide for the care of an animal alive during the settlor's lifetime. The trust terminates upon the death of the animal or, if the trust was created to provide for the care of more than one animal alive during the settlor's lifetime, upon the death of the last surviving animal.
Florida Trust - Trust for care of an animal	FL ST § 736.0408 (based on UTC § 408) Eff. 7/1/2007	This Florida statute provides that a trust may be created to provide for the care of an animal alive during the settlor's lifetime. The trust terminates on the death of the animal or, if the trust was created to provide for the care of more than one animal alive during the settlor's lifetime, on the death of the last surviving animal.
Georgia Trust for the care of an animal; creation; termination	GA ST § 53-12-28 Eff. 7/1/2010	This Georgia statute provides that a trust may be created to provide for the care of an animal that is alive during the settlor's lifetime. The trust shall terminate upon the death of such animal or, if the trust was created to provide for the care of more than one animal alive during the settlor's lifetime, upon the death of the last surviving animal.

State	Citation	Summary
Hawaii Trusts - Trusts for domestic or pet animals.	HI ST § 560:7-501 (based on UPC § 2-907) Eff. 6/24/2005	This statute represents Hawaii's pet trust law. The law provides that a pet trust is a valid purpose for a trust, and that such instruments are to be liberally construed to carry out the intent of the pet owner. Extrinsic evidence is admissible to prove the transferor's intent. Other aspects include an order for disbursement of remaining assets and a section that excludes these trusts from Hawaii's rule against perpetuities law.
Idaho Purpose trusts	ID ST § 15-7-601 Eff. 7/1/2005	This Idaho statute represents Idaho's relevant pet trust law. Although the law does not refer to a pet trust, it provides that a person may create a "purpose trust." This trust does not require a beneficiary and may instead just name a person to enforce the trust.
Illinois Trusts - Trusts for domestic or pet animals.	IL ST CH 760 § 5/15.2 (based on UPC § 2-907) Eff. 1/1/2005	This Illinois law represents the state's pet trust law. The law states that a trust to care for one or more designated domestic animals is valid and terminates upon the death of the last named animal. Such trusts are to be liberally construed under the law and extrinsic evidence is admissible to prove a transferor's intent.
Indiana Trust - Trust to provide for care of an animal alive during settlor's lifetime	IN ST 30-4-2-18 Eff. 7/1/2005	This Indiana statute provides that a trust for an animal terminates upon the death of the animal or upon death of last surviving animal alive during settlor's lifetime. Property of a trust authorized by this section may be applied only to the trust's intended use, except to the extent the court determines that the value of the trust property exceeds the amount required for the trust's intended use.
Iowa Trusts - Honorary trusts - trusts for pets	IA ST § 633A.2105 Eff. 2005	This Iowa statute allows for the creation of a trust for the continuing care of an animal living at the settlor's death (note that the actual text does not state "domestic" or "pet" animal). This type of trust, allowed generally through the provisions for lawful noncharitable trusts, is valid for up to twenty-one years, whether or not the terms of the trust contemplate a longer duration. The trust terminates when no living animal is covered by its terms.
Kansas Trusts - Trust for care of animal	KS ST § 58a-408 (based on UTC § 408) Eff. 1/1/2003	This Kansas statute provides that a trust may be created to provide for the care of an animal alive during the settlor's lifetime (note that it does not state "domestic" or "pet" animal). The trust terminates upon the death of the animal or, if the trust was created to provide for the care of more than one animal alive during the settlor's lifetime, upon the death of the last surviving animal. Property of a trust authorized by this section may be applied only to its intended use, except to the extent the court determines that the value of the trust property exceeds the amount required for the intended use.

State	Citation	Summary
Kentucky		No statute on pet trusts.
Louisiana		No statute on pet trusts.
Maine Trusts - Trust for care of animal.	ME ST T. 18-B § 408 (based on UTC § 408) Eff. 7/1/2005	This statute represents Maine's pet trust law, and provides that a trust may be created to provide for the care of an animal alive during the settlor's lifetime. The trust terminates upon the death of the animal or, if the trust was created to provide for the care of more than one animal alive during the settlor's lifetime, upon the death of the last surviving animal.
Maryland Trusts for care of animals	MD EST & TRST § 14-112 (based on UTC § 408) Eff. 10/1/2009	This Maryland statute provides that a trust may be created to provide for the care of an animal alive during the lifetime of the settlor. The trust terminates when the last animal subject to the trust dies. The property of the trust may only be used for the intended purpose of the trust (i.e., taking care of the animal) unless the court determines that the value exceeds the amount required for care.
Massachusetts Act relative to trusts for the care of animals	Mass. Laws ch. 203, § 3C Eff. 4/7/2011	This Massachusetts statute provides that a trust for the care of one or more animals is valid. Unless the trust provides otherwise, it will terminate on the death of the animal or animals for which it was created. The statute permits payment of reasonable trustee fees and expenses of administration, and also provides that the court may reduce the amount of property held by the trust if it substantially exceeds what is required for the intended use. It also provides an order of priority of distribution of unexpended trust property on termination of the trust. The statute permits the court to name a trustee if one was not named in the instrument, or to transfer the property to another trustee if necessary to carry out the settlor's intent and the intended use of the trust. It also provides a list of persons who can enforce the intended use of the trust principal or income. The custody of the animal may be transferred to the trustee by the settlor of the trust, or the custodian of the animal, either when the trust is created or as some time thereafter.

State	Citation	Summary
Michigan Honorary trust; trusts for pets	M. C. L. A. 700.2722 (based on UPC § 2-907) Eff. 4/1/2010	This Michigan statute provides that a trust for the care of a designated domestic or pet animal is valid (these trusts follow the terms for non-charitable trusts, and thus can be of a duration of up to 21 years). The trust terminates when no living animal is covered by the trust. Extrinsic evidence is admissible to prove the transferor's intent and the court may reduce the amount of the property transferred if it determines that that amount substantially exceeds the amount required for the intended use.
Minnesota		No statute on pet trusts.
Mississippi		No statute on pet trusts.
Missouri Trust for care of animal	MO ST 456.4-408 (based on UTC § 408) Eff. 2004	This Missouri statute represents the state's pet trust law. The law provides that a trust may be created to provide for the care of an animal alive during the settlor's lifetime. The trust terminates upon the death of the animal or, if the trust was created to provide for the care of more than one animal alive during the settlor's lifetime, upon the death of the last surviving animal.
Montana Trusts - Honorary trusts - trusts for pets	MT ST 72-2-1017 (based on UPC § 2-907) Eff. 1993 Amended 1995	This Montana statute states that a trust for the care of a designated domestic or pet animal is valid (but for no longer than 21 years, even if the trust provides for a longer term). The trust terminates when no living animal is covered by the trust. Extrinsic evidence is admissible in determining the transferor's intent. Except as expressly provided otherwise in the trust instrument, no portion of the principal or income may be converted to the use of the trustee or to any use other than for the trust's purposes or for the benefit of a covered animal. A court may reduce the amount of the property transferred if it determines that that amount substantially exceeds the amount required for the intended use.
Nebraska Trusts - Trust for care of animal	NE ST § 30-3834 (based on UTC § 408) Eff. 1/1/2005	This statute represents Nebraska's pet trust law. The law provides that a trust may be created to provide for the care of an animal alive during the settlor's lifetime. The trust terminates upon the death of the animal or, if the trust was created to provide for the care of more than one animal alive during the settlor's lifetime, upon the death of the last surviving animal.
Nevada Trusts - Validity of trust providing for care of one or more animals	NV ST 163.0075 Eff. 10/1/2001	This Nevada statute allows for a trust created for the care of one or more animals that are alive at the time of the settlor's death (note the statute does not state "domestic" or "pet" animal). Such a trust terminates upon the death of all animals covered by the terms of the trust. It further provides that a settlor's expression of intent must be liberally construed in favor of the creation of such a trust.

State	Citation	Summary
New Hampshire Trusts - Trust for Care of Animal	NH ST § 564-B:4-408 (based on UTC § 408) Eff. 10/1/2004	This statute represents New Hampshire's pet trust law. The law provides that a trust may be created to provide for the care of an animal alive during the settlor's lifetime. The trust terminates upon the death of the animal or, if the trust was created to provide for the care of more than one animal alive during the settlor's lifetime, upon the death of the last surviving animal.
New Jersey Trusts - Trusts for care of domesticated animals	NJ ST 3B:11-38 Eff. 7/1/2001	This New Jersey statute provides that a trust for the care of a domesticated animal is valid. Trusts under this section terminate when no living animal is covered by the trust, or at the end of 21 years, whichever occurs earlier.
New Mexico § 45-2-907 Honorary trusts; trusts for pets; § 46A-4-408. Trust for care of animal	NM ST §§ 45-2-907; 46A-4-408 (based on UTC § 408) Eff. 7/1/2003	New Mexico has two statutes that represent the state's relevant pet trust laws. The first law enacted, Section 45-2-907, was adopted in 1995, and provides that a trust for the care of a designated domestic or pet animal is valid. The trust terminates when no living animal is covered by the trust (but no longer than 21 years). A court may reduce the amount of the property transferred, if it determines that amount substantially exceeds the amount required for the intended use. The trust is to be liberally construed to effect its purpose and extrinsic evidence is admissible to prove the transferor's intent. The second statute, Section 46A-4-408, was adopted in 2003, and did not repeal the previous pet trust law. The new section follows the language of the Uniform Trust Code and simply states that a trust for the care of an animal alive during the settlor's lifetime is valid. The trust terminates upon the death of the last animal named and any excess trust property is distributed to the settlor, if living, or his or her successors in interest.
New York Trusts for pets	NY EST POW & TRST § 7-8.1 Eff. 1996 Amended 2010	This New York statute provides that a trust for the care of a designated domestic or pet animal is valid. Such trust shall terminate when no living animal is covered by the trust, or at the end of twenty-one years, whichever occurs earlier. Upon termination, the trustee shall transfer the unexpended trust property as directed in the trust instrument or, if there are no such directions in the trust instrument, the property shall pass to the estate of the grantor. A court may reduce the amount of the property transferred if it determines that amount substantially exceeds the amount required for the intended use.

State	Citation	Summary
North Carolina Trusts - Trusts for pets	NC ST § 36C-4-408 - replaces NC ST § 36A-147 (1995) (based on UPC § 2-907) Eff. 11/1/2006	This North Carolina provides that a trust for the care of one or more designated domestic or pet animals alive at the time of creation of the trust is valid. Further, no portion of the principal or income may be converted to the use of the trustee or to any use other than for the benefit of the designated animal or animals. The trust terminates upon the death of the animal named or the last surviving animal named in the trust.
North Dakota Trust - Trust for care of animal	ND ST 59-12-08 (based on UTC § 408) Eff. 8/1/2007	This North Dakota statute provides that a trust may be created to provide for the care of an animal alive during the settlor's lifetime. The trust terminates upon the death of the animal or, if the trust was created to provide for the care of more than one animal alive during the settlor's lifetime, upon the death of the last surviving animal.
Ohio Trust - Trust for care of animal	OH ST § 5804.08 (based on UTC § 408) Eff. 1/1/2007	This Ohio statute provides that a trust may be created to provide for the care of an animal alive during the settlor's lifetime. The trust terminates upon the death of the animal or, if the trust was created to provide for the care of more than one animal alive during the settlor's lifetime, upon the death of the last surviving animal.
Oklahoma Validity of a trust for the care of domestic or pet animals.	OK ST T. 60 § 199 Eff. 8/27/2010	This Oklahoma statute provides that a trust for the care of designated domestic or pet animals is valid and terminates when no living animal is covered by the trust. If no trustee is named, the court shall appoint one.
Oregon Trusts - Pet Trust	OR REV ST § 130.185 (based on UTC § 408) Eff. 1/1/2006	This statute comprises Oregon's Pet Trust. Under the law, a trust may be created to provide for the care of one or more animals that are alive during the settlor's lifetime. The trust terminates upon the death of the animal or, if the trust was created to provide for the care of more than one animal, upon the death of the last surviving animal.
Pennsylvania Trust - Trust for care of animal	PA ST 20 Pa.C.S.A. § 7738 (based on UTC § 408) Eff. 11/4/2006	This Pennsylvania statute provides that a trust may be created to provide for the care of an animal alive during the settlor's lifetime. The trust terminates upon the death of the animal or, if the trust was created to provide for the care of more than one animal alive during the settlor's lifetime, upon the death of the last surviving animal.

State	Citation	Summary
Rhode Island Trusts - Trust for care of animals.	RI ST § 4-23-1 Eff. 7/19/2005	This Rhode Island statute provides that a trust may be created to provide for the care of an animal alive during the settlor's lifetime. The trust terminates upon the death of the animal, or if the trust was created to provided for the care of more than one animal alive during the settlor's lifetime, upon the death of the last surviving animal. The statute includes a distribution schedule for any remaining trust property and also states that such trusts are to be liberally construed to carry out the transferor's intent.
South Carolina Trust - Trust for care of animal	SC ST § 62-7-408 (based on UTC § 408) Eff. 1/1/2006	This South Carolina statute provides that a trust may be created to provide for the care of an animal or animals alive or in gestation during the settlor's lifetime, whether or not alive at the time the trust is created. The trust terminates upon the death of the last surviving animal.
South Dakota Trust - Trust for care of designated animal; Provisions governing trusts for specific purposes selected by trustee and for care of animals	SD ST § 55-1-21 through 23 (based on UPC § 2-907) Approved 2/22/2006	This South Dakota statute provides that a trust for an animal terminates when no living animal is covered by the trust. A governing instrument shall be liberally construed to bring the transfer within this section.
Tennessee Trusts -Trust for care of animal	TN ST § 35-15-408 Eff. 7/1/2004, Amended eff. 4/12/2007	This Tennessee statute provides that a trust may be created to provide for the care of an animal alive during the settlor's lifetime. The trust terminates upon the death of the animal or, if the trust was created to provide for the care of more than one animal alive during the settlor's lifetime, upon the death of the last surviving animal. The trust may not be enforced for more than 90 years.
Texas Trusts - Creation, Validity, Modification, and Termination of Trusts.	TX PROPERTY § 112.037 Eff. 1/1/2006	This Texas statute comprises the state's pet trust law. A trust may be created to provide for the care of an animal alive during the settlor's lifetime. The trust terminates on the death of the animal or, if the trust is created to provide for the care of more than one animal alive during the settlor's lifetime, on the death of the last surviving animal. The law also provides a distribution schedule for the trust's remaining assets.
Utah Trusts - Honorary trusts - Trusts for pets	UT ST § 75-2-1001 (based on UPC § 2-907) Eff. 7/1/1998 Amended 2003	This Utah statute provides that a trust for the care of a designated domestic or pet animal is valid. The trust terminates when no living animal is covered by the trust. Trusts under this section shall be liberally construed to presume against the merely precatory or honorary nature of the disposition, and to carry out the general intent of the transferor.

State	Citation	Summary
Vermont Trust for care of animal	Vt. Stat. §14A-408 (based on UTC § 408) Eff. 7/1/2009	This Vermont statute provides that a trust may be created to provide for the care of an animal alive during the settlor's lifetime. The trust terminates on the death of the last surviving animal for which it was created. The trust may be enforced by someone appointed under the trust or by the probate court if the trust does not appoint anyone. Anyone having an interest in the animal's welfare may request the court to appoint someone to enforce the trust or remove a person appointed. The statute permits the probate court to limit the amount in the trust if it exceeds the amount required for its intended use. Unless the trust provides otherwise, the excess is be distributed to the settlor, if living, and if not then to the settlor's successors in interest.
Virginia Trusts - Trust for care of animal.	VA ST § 55-544.08 (based on UTC § 408) Eff. 7/1/2006	This Virginia statute provides that a trust may be created to provide for the care of an animal alive during the settlor's lifetime. The trust terminates upon the death of the animal or, if the trust was created to provide for the care of more than one animal alive during the settlor's lifetime, upon the death of the last surviving animal.
Washington Trusts - Animals	WA ST 11.118.005 - 11.118.110 (based on UPC § 2-907) Eff. 2001	The purpose of this chapter is to recognize and validate certain trusts that are established for the benefit of animals (nonhuman animal with vertebrae). The trust can be for one or more animals provided they are individually identified or labeled in the instrument so that they may be easily identified. Unless otherwise provided in the trust instrument or in this chapter, the trust will terminate when no animal that is designated as a beneficiary of the trust remains living.
West Virginia		No statute on pet trusts.
Wisconsin Trust - Honorary trusts; cemetery trusts.	WI ST 701.11 Eff. 1969	This statute represents Wisconsin's pet trust law. While not a specific pet trust law, Wisconsin's law states that a settlor may form a general honorary trust with no ascertainable human beneficiary provided it is not for a "capricious purpose."
Wyoming Trust - Trust for care of animal	WY ST § 4-10-409 (based on UTC § 408) Eff. 7/1/2003	This statute represents Wyoming's pet trust law. The law provides that a trust may be created to provide for the care of an animal alive during the settlor's lifetime. The trust terminates upon the death of the last animal named in the trust.

PET CARD

WALLET CARD FOR PET OWNER

In case of emergency, please call my pets' backup caregivers (see reverse side).

_____
Name of pet owner

_____
Address of pet owner

Names of Pets   Type of Animal

_____

_____

_____

Fold

- -

EMERGENCY CAREGIVERS FOR MY PETS

Name	Daytime Tel.	Evening Tel.

Name	Daytime Tel.	Evening Tel.

Name	Daytime Tel.	Evening Tel.

If you cannot reach any of the above, please call my (check one):

☐ Pet Sitter   ☐ Boarding Kennel   ☐ Veterinarian

Name	Daytime Tel.	Evening Tel.

This page intentionally left blank.

SIGN FOR RESIDENCE OF PET OWNER

Attention!
Police & Fire
PETS LIVE HERE!

_____Dogs   Names _____

_____Cats   Names _____

_____Other   Names _____

More information in envelope on other side of door.
Thank you for taking care of our pets!

This page intentionally left blank.

PET INFORMATION SHEET

1. INFORMATION ABOUT THE PET OWNER(S)

Pet Owner #1:

Name

Address

City, State, Zip Code

Email Address

Home Tel.   Work Tel.   Cell phone:

If there is a second pet owner, please complete the following:

Pet Owner #2:

Name

Address

City, State, Zip Code

Email Address

Home Tel.   Work Tel.   Cell phone:

2. INFORMATION ABOUT YOUR PET

Pet's name:

Type of pet:

☐ Dog   ☐ Indoor Cat   ☐ Outdoor Cat   ☐ Bird   ☐ Horse   ☐ Other (specify):

Approximate date of birth: Male ☐   Female ☐

What breed?   Microchip #

Does your pet have any identifying marks? No ☐   Yes ☐

Tatoos (describe)

Scars (describe)   Unique coloring (describe)

Please attach one or more photos of your pet.

Does your pet have any medical condition that requires special medical treatment? If so, describe:

Does your pet require a special exercise routine? If so, describe:

Feeding schedule:

Brand and type of pet food(s):

How much and how many times per day?

What time of day?

Any medications?   Any supplements?

3. YOUR PET'S DAILY SCHEDULE AND HABITS

What time does your pet wake up?   When is bedtime?

How many hours a day does your pet sleep?

Where does your pet like to sleep?

Are there any special activities during the day?

Any favorite type of petting or brushing?

Any secrets to calm your pet if frightened or aggressive?

Does your pet travel well in a car?   Will your pet walk on a leash?

Is there anything you would want your pet's caregiver to know about your pet's behavior (favorite toys, likes and dislikes, fears, etc.)?

4. PET INSURANCE

Do you have pet care insurance? Yes ☐   No ☐

If so, please provide:

Name of insurance company:

Policy number for this pet:

Phone number:

Where is the policy located?

What is the annual premium? $ Due date:

5. PET'S MEDICAL INFORMATION

Briefly describe your pet's medical history (attach additional sheets if necessary):

Where can a caregiver find a complete medical history?

How many times per year should your pet be taken to the veterinarian for routine visits?

Name of veterinarian:

Address:

City, State, Zip Code:

Email Address:

Office Tel.   Cell phone:

If your veterinarian is not available, do you have a backup veterinarian?

If so, please provide:

Name of backup veterinarian:

Address:

City, State, Zip Code:

Email Address:

Office Tel.   Cell phone:

6. EMERGENCY MEDICAL FACILITY

Do you prefer a specific animal hospital or emergency care facility in case of emergency?

If so, please provide:

Name of emergency pet care facility:

Address:

City, State, Zip Code:

Email Address:

Office Tel.   Cell phone:

7. PET WALKER INFORMATION

Do you use someone to walk your pet? If so, please provide:

Name:

Address:

City, State, Zip Code:

Email Address:

Home tel.   Work Tel.   Cell phone:

Is there a regular schedule for that person's services? If so, what is it?

Rate of pay: $ per

Does your pet walker have a key to your house or apartment?   Yes ☐ No ☐

8. BOARDING FACILITY

Do you use a particular boarding facility for your pet when necessary? If so, please provide:

Name of boarding facility:

Address:

City, State, Zip Code:

Email Address:

Office Tel.   Cell phone:

9. EMERGENCY COORDINATOR

In case of an emergency where you are not available, who should be contacted to coordinate getting your caregiver to step in? This could be a member of your family, someone you work with, a friend or a neighbor.

Name:

Address:

Home Tel.   Work Tel.   Cell phone:

In case that person cannot be reached, is there another person who should be contacted as a backup? If so, please provide that person's contact information:

Name

Address

Home Tel.   Work Tel.   Cell phone:

PET TRUST DRAFTING CHECKLIST

The following questionnaire addresses issues involved in creation of a Pet Trust. After having read the book, you should be ready to answer these questions, or discuss them with your attorney. Your Pet Trust will most likely be revocable, which means that you can change it any time during your lifetime and so long as you are legally competent. Please also complete a Pet Information Sheet (Appendix D) for each pet.

This checklist is necessarily a work in progress. Readers of this book may request a complimentary copy of the latest version of this checklist in MS Word format by emailing inquiries@carobtreepress.com.

1. INFORMATION ABOUT THE PET OWNER(S)

Pet Owner #1:

Address:

City, State, Zip Code

Email Address:

Home Tel.   Work Tel.   Cell phone:

If there is a second pet owner, please complete the following:

Pet Owner #2:

Name:

Address:

City, State, Zip Code

Email Address:

Home Tel.   Work Tel.   Cell phone:

Pets to be covered (also attach completed copies of the Pet Information Sheet, one for each pet):

Should the Pet Trust be drafted to cover any other pets you may own at such time as you are unable to care for your pets?   Yes ☐   No ☐

If you have more than one pet, do you feel strongly that they should all live together in one home or facility?

Yes ☐   No ☐

If you have to move to a nursing home, assisted living or other facility do you want to have your pets live with you while you are in the facility?   Yes ☐   No ☐

Do you have any preference for a particular nursing home or assisted living facility?

Yes ☐   No ☐   If so, please indicate the name, location, and phone number of the facility.

If you are in a facility which only permits pets to visit but not to stay, do you want to direct your pet's caregiver to have the pet visit you?   Yes ☐   No ☐

If so, how often?

    ☐   As often as possible, in the judgment of the pet's caregiver

    ☐   No less than once a week

    ☐   Other (please describe):

Your pet's caregiver will need to determine when he or she will be authorized to start taking care of your pets. One way will be if you yourself notify the caregiver that you no longer consider yourself able to take care of your pets.

However, if you do not do that, we suggest that someone else also be required to make that determination with the caregiver. If you agree with that suggestion, then we recommend you designate one of two other people to make that determination:

Pet's caregiver + one of the following people:

#1 Name

Address:

City, State, Zip Code

Email Address:

Home Tel.   Work Tel.   Cell phone:

#2 Name

Address:

City, State, Zip Code

Email Address:

Home Tel.   Work Tel.   Cell phone:

Having your pet's caregiver take care of your pets does not mean that you will necessarily be legally incapacitated. Rather, it only indicates that you are physically unable to care for your pets.

2. FUNDING OF YOUR PET TRUST

Please provide your attorney a copy of any worksheet you used to determine how much money should be set aside in the Pet Trust.

When do you intend to "fund" your Pet Trust, i.e., put money or other property into it? You may fund it entirely when the trust is set up, entirely after your death, or some when it is set up and the balance after your death.

☐   At the time the Pet Trust is set up $ _____

☐   After your death $ _____

Do you want these amounts indexed based on the Consumer Price Index? (That will cause the dollar amounts to automatically adjust based on increases in the cost of living.)

Yes ☐   No ☐

What will be the sources of funding?

☐   Your general bank accounts or other assets

☐   A special bank account in your name. If a bank account will be designated for this purpose:

Name of bank:

Location:

Account number:

☐   Life insurance

Insurance Company:

Policy Number:

Death benefit to be used to fund the Pet Trust (need not be 100% of the death benefit under a given policy).   It can be a percentage or a fixed dollar amount.

☐ $ _____   ☐ _____% of death benefits

3. CHOICE OF PET'S CAREGIVER

Some people will have the pet's caregiver take care of both the financial aspects of the Pet Trust and the pet's care. Others will designate two separate people, one to take care of the pet (the pet's caregiver), and another to handle the finances (the Trustee).

Indicate whom you would like to designate as your pet's **caregiver**; we will discuss a possible **Trustee** later. *If different caregivers are to take care of different pets, please provide information on a separate sheet.*

Name of Pet Caregiver:

Address:

City, State, Zip Code

Email Address:

Home Tel.   Work Tel.   Cell phone:

It is a good idea to name several people as successors to your pet's caregiver, if for some reason your first choice of pet caregiver is unable to care for your pets, resigns, dies, or fails to render proper care for your pets. If you can, please provide up to three Successor pet caregivers:

Successor Pet Caregiver #1

Address:

City, State, Zip Code

Email Address:

Home Tel.   Work Tel.   Cell phone:

Successor Pet Caregiver #2

Address:

City, State, Zip Code

Email Address:

Home Tel.   Work Tel.   Cell phone:

Successor Pet Caregiver #3

Address:

City, State, Zip Code

Email Address:

Home Tel.   Work Tel.   Cell phone:

If none of your pet caregivers and successors mentioned above can serve, what would you like to be done with your pets?

☐   Have the Trustee of your Pet Trust appoint a caregiver (this assumes you have nominated a person other than your caregiver to handle the finances).

☐   Give your pets to a pet sanctuary or animal shelter. If so, please specify:

Name and location of pet sanctuary or animal shelter

Tel.

☐   Give your pets to your veterinarian for placement.

☐   Other (specify)

4. CHOICE OF TRUSTEE

People sometimes want to divide the day-to-day responsibility of taking care of the pets (the function of the pet's caregiver) from the responsibility of distributing money in the Pet Trust for the pet's care (the function of the Trustee). If you have questions about this, see Chapter 3 and discuss this issue with your attorney.

If you have decided to divide up these responsibilities, whom would you like to serve as **Trustee**?

Trustee Name:

Address:

City, State, Zip Code

Email Address:

Home Tel.   Work Tel.   Cell phone:

If you have decided to have a separate person as Trustee, it is a good idea to name several people as successors to your Trustee, if for some reason your Trustee decides to resign, dies, or becomes disabled. If you can, please provide up to three Successor Trustees:

Successor Trustee #1:

Address:

City, State, Zip Code

Email Address:

Home Tel.   Work Tel.   Cell phone:

Successor Trustee #2:

Address:

City, State, Zip Code

Email Address:

Home Tel.   Work Tel.   Cell phone:

Successor Trustee #3:

Address:

City, State, Zip Code

Email Address:

Home Tel.   Work Tel.   Cell phone:

If you have decided to have a separate Trustee, that person would watch over the caregiver, to make sure that your pets are being given proper care. Do you want the Trustee to check in on your pet periodically?

No ☐   Yes ☐   If so, how often?

5. PAYMENT OF CARE EXPENSES

If you have decided you want to have a separate Trustee, how much and how often do you want the Trustee to distribute to the caregiver for your pet's care (a base amount, subject to additional distributions for for extraordinary expenses)?

☐   Fixed amount: $_____   ☐ Weekly   ☐ Monthly   ☐ Annually

☐   Allow the Trustee to give the caregiver a debit card to charge against the Pet Trust account

☐   Leave the amount in the discretion of the Trustee

6. COMPENSATION ISSUES

Do you want to pay your pet's **caregiver** for taking care of your pets?   No ☐   Yes ☐

If so, how much and how often should that person be paid?

☐   Fixed amount: $_____ ☐ Weekly   ☐ Monthly   ☐ Annually

☐   Leave the amount in the discretion of the Trustee

Do you want to pay your **Trustee** for handling the financial aspects of your Trust?   No ☐   Yes ☐

If so, how much and how often should that person be paid?

☐   Fixed amount: $_____ ☐ Weekly   ☐ Monthly   ☐ Annually

☐   A "reasonable" amount, but in the discretion of the Trustee

If you have indicated any fixed dollar amounts above, do you want those amounts to be adjusted for inflation?

No ☐   Yes ☐

If you are leaving the determination of the amount the Trustee will pay himself or herself to be decided by the Trustee, would you like to have that subject to the approval of a third party?

No ☐   Yes ☐

If so, we would recommend that you appoint a **Trust Protector**, to serve without compensation, or with only nominal compensaton, to oversee the Trustee and the pet's caregiver. *However, check with your attorney to make sure your state law allows appointment of a Trust Protector for a trust.* If it does, and if you want someone to have to approve the compensation of the Trustee, whom would you like to serve as initial Trust Protector?

Trust Protector:

Address:

City, State, Zip Code

Email Address:

Home Tel.   Work Tel.   Cell phone:

If you have a Trust Protector, it is a good idea to name several people as Successor Trust Protectors, if for some reason your Trust Protector decides to resign, dies, or becomes disabled. If you can, please provide up to three Successor Trust Protectors:

Successor Trust Protector #1:

Address:

City, State, Zip Code

Email Address:

Home Tel.   Work Tel.   Cell phone:

Successor Trust Protector #2:

Address:

City, State, Zip Code

Email Address:

Home Tel.   Work Tel.   Cell phone:

Successor Trust Protector #3:

Address:

City, State, Zip Code

Email Address:

Home Tel.   Work Tel.   Cell phone:

The Trust Protector will have the power to enforce your Pet Trust and to ensure that, except for reasonable, permitted compensation, the funds are being spent only for the benefit of your pets.

You can give the Trust Protector a wide range of powers. Please indicate which of the following specific powers you would like to give to the Trust Protector. If you have any question about any of them, please ask your attorney:

☐ The power to remove any pet caregiver or Trustee if the person serving is unable or unwilling to act in the best interest of your pets.

☐ The power to name a successor pet caregiver or Successor Trustee there is no one listed in your Pet Trust who is willing and able to serve.

☐ The power to resolve deadlocks or differences of opinion between the pet's caregiver and the Trustee.

☐ The power to block or veto distributions from the Pet Trust, or to encourage distributions from the Pet Trust.

☐ The power to veto investment decisions of the Trustee.

☐ The power to terminate the Pet Trust if it appears to the Trust Protector that there are insufficient funds or the cost to administer the Pet Trust is excessive in view of the available funds.

7. MEDICAL SUPERVISION AND PET INSURANCE

The pet's caregiver should take your pets to the veterinarian indicated in the Pet Information Sheet at the frequency indicated. The reports of these visits should be sent to the then acting Trustee and Trust Protector, if any.

Do you want to authorize your Trustee to purchase pet insurance? No ☐ Yes ☐

If so, do you have any specific types of pet insurance you want or do no want to be purchased? If so, please provide details.

Do you have any preferred companies, or companies from which you would prefer that the Trustee not purchase pet insurance? If so, please provide details.

8. END OF LIFE ISSUES CONCERNING YOUR PETS

If your pet has a serious accident or becomes seriously ill, are there any circumstances under which you want your pet euthanized?   No ☐   Yes ☐

If yes, do you want to impose any of the following guidelines for when your pet should be euthanized?

☐   If your pet's **veterinarian** determines that your pet has a serious or terminal medical condition, which cannot be resolved, and that the pet will be in less pain as a result.

☐   If **two veterinarians**, including the pet's regular veterinarian, make the above determination.

☐   If the **caregiver** you designate for your pet makes the above determination, *based on the recommendation of the number of veterinarians indicated above.*

☐   If the **Trustee** of your Pet Trust makes the above determination, *based on the recommendation of the number of veterinarians indicated above.*

☐   If the **Trust Protector**, if any, nominated under your Pet Trust makes the above determination, *based on the recommendation of the number of veterinarians indicated above.*

☐   Other (please specify):

Some people want safeguards against their pet's caregiver substituting other pets for their pets, or causing the deaths of their pets, so that the funds in the Pet Trust pass to the remainder beneficiary.

Do you want your pets to have DNA testing after their death, with the results sent to all persons named in the Pet Trust, so that it can be determined that these were your pets?   No ☐   Yes ☐

Do you want your pets to have a necropsy (autopsy) to determine their cause of death?   No ☐   Yes ☐

Some people are concerned that terminating a Pet Trust too soon after a pet goes missing encourages improper behavior on behalf of the pet's caregiver.   Do you want to impose a five year waiting period after a pet goes missing, before terminating the Pet Trust?   No ☐   Yes ☐

After the death of a pet, how do you want the remains disposed of?

☐ Cremation   ☐ Burial   ☐ Other (specify)

9. DISTRIBUTION OF REMAINING FUNDS UPON TERMINATION OF PET TRUST

On the death of all of your pets subject to the Pet Trust, the trust will terminate, and any remaining funds will be distributed according to your instructions.

You can leave the funds to those people who are serving as your pet's caregiver, Trustee, and/or Trust Protector at the time the trust is terminated; to a nursing home or assisted living facility at which you may have stayed and which permitted your pets to stay with you; to animal care or animal rights organizations or other charities; to beneficiaries under your main estate plan; or to anyone else you choose.

It is probably best to do this by indicating a percentage of the balance to each person or organization to whom you want a distribution to be made. Please indicate below the percentages, from 0% to 100% (the total must be 100%).

_____%   Pet's caregiver

_____%   Trustee

_____%   Trust Protector

_____%   Nursing home or assisted living facility

_____%   Animal care or animal rights organizations (please attach a separate list with names, addresses and percentages)

_____%   Other charitable organizations (please attach a separate list with names, addresses and percentages)

_____%   Beneficiaries under your estate plan (please attach a separate list with names, addresses and percentages)

_____%   Others (please attach a separate list with names, addresses and percentages)

100%   Total